The *Other* Side of *Organized*

The *Other* Side of
Organized

Finding Balance Between Chaos and Perfection

LINDA SAMUELS, CPO-CD®

Oh, So Publishing!

Croton on Hudson, New York

PUBLISHED BY OH, SO PUBLISHING!

Croton on Hudson, New York

www.ohsopublishing.com

Edited by The Threepenny Editor

Cover and book design by *the*BookDesigners

Cartoons by Richard Rockwell and Linda Samuels

Author photo by Allison Eve Samuels

First Edition

ISBN 978-0-9841699-0-0

THIS BOOK IS DEDICATED
WITH ALL MY HEART TO THE LOVES OF MY LIFE:
Steve, Allison and Cassie

Contents

Acknowledgements

WRITING THIS BOOK has been on my "list" for years. I needed the time to marinate the ideas and meet the amazing people whose lives have touched mine. I am thankful for their love, encouragement, conversations, wisdom and trust. My heartfelt appreciation goes to all of my family, friends, clients and colleagues for sharing your wonderful selves with me. I am honored to have you in my life.

Producing this book would not have been accomplished without the help from an incredible team including book coach Julie Trelstad; editor Sarah Cypher; designers at *the*BookDesigners; print staff at Lightning Source; manuscript reviewers Sheila Delson, Barry Izsak, Ellen Littman, Stacey Weglein, Wilma Machover, Allison Samuels and Steve Samuels; logo designers Ron Romain and Joe Crabtree; and artist Richard Rockwell. Thank you so much for your role in helping me bring this project to fruition.

My deepest gratitude for my husband Steve and daughters Allison and Cassie for your patience, love, encouragement, help and extra hugs as you joined me on this journey. Words cannot adequately express my love for each of you. Thank you for sharing this incredible adventure with me.

Introduction

"Live in each season as it passes; breathe the air, drink the drink, taste the fruit." —HENRY DAVID THOREAU

EAST COAST LIVING has greatly influenced the way I think about life. Each season is another chance to examine goals, rethink strategies and negotiate life's balance. The unmistakable transformation of scenery four times a year inspires me to embrace change: These seasonal cues nudge me to reevaluate how things are going, what needs improving, or what is working so well that it should stay as-is. The seeds for this book developed from reflections during exactly those times, the change of seasons.

Organizing is something that comes to me easily and naturally. Early on, people noticed my abilities and said I appeared to have been "born organized." I was one of those kids that couldn't wait to purchase new school supplies so that I could set up my three-ring binder. I derived great pleasure from lining up the nail polish bottles in color order. After returning from trick-or-treating, I loved sorting the Halloween candy by type into small bags. I never really thought much about my joy of order. It was just what I did and it brought me enormous satisfaction.

As an adult, I recognized that the very skill I took for granted, other people struggled with on a regular basis. In some cases, their lack of organization created great stress and strife in their lives and relationships. In 1993, when I identified the possibility of being able to affect people's lives in a positive way by sharing my skills, I launched Oh, So Organized! to work with clients who wanted my help. I am deeply grateful to be part of their lives.

Simultaneously with the growth of my organizing business, my husband and I spent those same years raising our two daughters from babies to teenagers. Our girls have taught me much more than I've taught them: We grew up together and they have profoundly influenced how I feel about living, organizing, and creating life balance.

The Other Side of Organized is written for you. Whether you consider yourself chronically disorganized, highly organized or somewhere in between, my hope is after reading this book you will feel inspired to pursue a level of organization and balance that works for you. This book's individual passages were written over many years. They have been organized by season and themes. While they can be read sequentially, some can also be read individually according to your needs. Many of my colleagues have written excellent "how-to" books on organizing. I have included some practical suggestions, but my primary focus is on sharing ideas about organizing and life balance.

There is a difference between organizing something and truly using order to live a fuller life. I encourage you to let the ideas that follow inspire you to create the life you desire. There is more to life than just organizing.

Every chapter begins with a cartoon inspired by our black lab, Norton. I collaborated with friend and artist Richard Rockwell to turn my concepts into a cartoon strip. Long before this book was published, the series appeared in my organizing newsletter. Several years ago, both Norton and Richard passed away. After I finalized the themes for the chapters in this book, I made an amazing discovery. We had created exactly twelve "Norton" cartoons that corresponded perfectly with the twelve chapters' themes in the book. Richard always wanted to illustrate my first book, so I am especially thrilled to include these strips. Even though Richard is no longer with us, his art and humor lives on.

I

Winter

*"The color of springtime is in the flowers,
the color of winter is in the imagination."*
—WARD ELLIOT HOUR

WINTER MARKS THE END OF ONE YEAR AND THE BEGINNING OF ANOTHER. AS THE WHITE SNOW COVERS THE GROUND, ITS QUIET INFUSES ME WITH A SENSE OF PEACE AND CALM. THE STILLNESS ALLOWS ME TO HEAR MYSELF THINK. DESPITE THE CHILL IN THE AIR, I FEEL HOPEFUL FOR THE OPPORTUNITY TO REFLECT AND BEGIN AGAIN.

ONE

Fresh Start

NORTON KNOWS

Second chances AND NEW BEGINNINGS LET US REEVALUATE WHAT'S IMPORTANT AND RESET OUR GOALS.

LIKE MANY PEOPLE, I have to do things multiple times until I get them right. I refer to this as the *trial and error* or *fail your way to success* path in life. Compassion for others and ourselves is essential because we can be unnecessarily judgmental during the journey.

Fortunately, life is forgiving and gives us ample opportunity to try again. Whether you choose to begin fresh tomorrow or next week, you have the ability to do so. Forgive yourself for what you didn't accomplish and just start again. It is normal to try and fail multiple times before succeeding. Be patient. Keep perspective as you think about your goals. Focus on what is important and on what you are passionate about.

Resolutions

Each day brings a new opportunity to begin again.

IN WINTER ESPECIALLY, I receive many calls from people who have made getting organized one of their New Year's resolutions. I empathize with the commitment it takes to change habits and attain goals.

One of my personal challenges has been trying to integrate regular exercise into my life. After many years of procrastinating, I finally began an exercise routine and experienced wonderful results. I felt healthier, stronger, less stressed, and proud to have conquered my multitude of excuses. I had some good ones too, like "I'm too tired," "I haven't seen my dog all day," or "I don't feel like putting on my sneakers."

For many months, I exercised regularly with much encouragement from my family and friends. Then slowly I stopped, until one day I realized that several months had elapsed since I'd worked out. One of my New Year's resolutions was to restart my routine. To help me stay committed, I repeated the words, "No excuses; just do it!"

Whatever your challenge is, be it exercising, getting organized, or something else, remember that you can overcome it with commitment, effort, and a few supporters cheering you on. Have compassion and forgive yourself. Tomorrow will be a new day that will bring a fresh start. Begin again.

Have compassion and forgive yourself. Tomorrow will be a new day that will bring a fresh start.

The Magic Wand
There is something magical about beginning a new year.

WINTER IS NOT just another season. It's a time to reflect, take a deep breath, and forgive yourself and others.

This special season reminds me of something a client once shared. She said, "I wish you had a magic wand. You could wave it and I'd be organized instantly!" Thoughts of *Mary Poppins* and *I Dream of Jeannie* came to mind. After we laughed, I told her I was sorry to disappoint her, but unfortunately, I didn't have a magic wand.

Even though no wand existed, I assured her that I was there to help her work a different kind of magic. It would take effort and commitment. There would be moments of ease and ones of challenge.

Just like the caterpillar that must struggle to emerge from its cocoon to become a butterfly, my client had to go through the organizing process to experience growth and to own the changes. The positive results she experienced after organizing felt magical, even without the wand.

In Hot Pursuit
Obsession can take over when pursuing a goal.

I'LL FESS UP. Once I get an idea of something I want to accomplish, I can act like a dog with a bone. My entire being gets energized and I won't let go until the goal is reached. My family will attest to the fact that there are times when I become obsessed—my desire to complete things is very strong. And because I know this about myself, I have to work diligently to maintain balance. This becomes especially challenging when I'm in the midst of a project. To support harmony during these times, it's critical that I get enough sleep, nutrition, hydration, fresh air, and social interaction. When any of these pieces are out of sync, I can easily become overwhelmed.

It's exciting to pursue and attain a goal. The challenge during those times is to maintain some semblance of balance with the rest of your life.

Write Your Goals

The effect of committing your goals to paper can have a profound influence on your life.

AS WINTER APPROACHED, I was energized with many ideas. December calendar entries pushed me to commit these thoughts to paper. Somehow, with the excitement of the holidays, time off, parties and family gatherings, I managed to glide right into January without having my personal goal-setting session. Instead, I completely enjoyed the unplanned time, the beautiful winter landscape, staying up late and sleeping even later. Instead of planning, I simply enjoyed the vacation time. As January first came and went, slight panic and even disappointment crept in. Why had I procrastinated? I was so busy having fun that I hadn't made time to pause, reflect and commit those goals to paper. My disappointment turned into forgiveness when I reminded myself that my "float" time was just as essential as the "planning" time. In the following weeks, I took the time to gather my thoughts on paper. That the deadline had been slightly postponed didn't matter.

The act of writing your annual goals is more powerful than you might imagine. I encourage you to try this simple technique. If you write your goals down, by the end of the year, you'll reflect back and amaze yourself with all you've accomplished.

Goal-setting

If you feel overwhelmed by creating too many goals, simplify and only commit to accomplishing a few this year.

JANUARY IS NATIONAL Get Organized Month. It's the ideal month to get inspired and set your goals. It's easy and very normal to let our goals float around in our heads. We use a lot of mental energy thinking about what we'd like to accomplish, yet we do not necessarily take action. An essential part of goal-setting is to actually commit your goals to paper. Find a way to write them down, using whichever method suits you best, be it the computer or otherwise. Do not skip this step, as it is essential ingredient for success.

Release your goals from your brain onto paper. Don't limit yourself. You can fine-tune your list later. If it's helpful, think about categorizing goals for each area of your life. Areas might include family, social, financial, personal development, physical health, professional, or spiritual.

Now that you are done with the *brain download*, take some time to look over your goals. If you have too many and you're feeling overwhelmed, then it's time to simplify. Select just a few and commit to accomplishing them this year. Some years are more productive than others. It takes a lot of energy to continually work towards something. There are times when we get tired or life's challenges interrupt our pursuits. There's nothing wrong with stretching yourself, but do take into account all that's happening in your life right now as you select which goals to pursue. To achieve the best possible outcome, consider the entire picture.

Once you've selected your goals, share them with others so that they can encourage you along the way. Many of us benefit from a cheerleader's positive energy. We like to know we're on the right track and that those close to us care about our success. Sharing your goals with others can be helpful in establishing accountability. Sometimes we need that extra push, knowing that another person is *watching* us. This type of relationship happens with many clients. During our sessions, we work on accomplishing their goals. My encouragement helps them move ahead. In between visits, they often continue working. When I see them the next time, we acknowledge their progress. The movement is not always in a forward direction, though: There are times when they struggle and take a few steps back. This is a normal part of the process. The goals are reset and we begin again.

Goal Size
Creating mini-goals can make your larger goals feel less overwhelming.

YOU MIGHT BE WONDERING if you should make small or large goals. It doesn't really matter. The idea is to commit to accomplishing something. A large goal could be "organize my entire house" or "write a book." A smaller goal might be "organize the kitchen junk drawer" or "write an outline for the book." Do not judge the size of your ideas as you're writing them down. You can always create mini-goals to make the larger goals less overwhelming. Creating mini-goals will probably be unnecessary, if the goal you choose is smaller.

New Clarity of Purpose

After going through tumultuous life events, our perspective can be altered, which enables us to move ahead at a different pace.

ONE DICTIONARY'S DEFINITION of *goal* is "the object of a person's ambition or effort." It implies nothing about the time you might need to achieve that goal, only that there is a destination in mind, which requires desire and determination to get there. The entire concept of "how long will it take?" is a fascinating one that clients often ask about. The "how long" factor depends on many variables. Time is affected by life circumstances, readiness for change, willingness to make commitments and tools or resources to achieve the goals.

I've noticed that when a person goes through a major life change such as the birth of a child, moving, new job, marriage, divorce, illness or loss of a loved one, the rate at which goals are achieved is escalated. During these shifts, life gets intense. There is no "normal." There is a lot of stress as the person negotiates their new patterns and emotions. The familiar has completely changed. Once the crisis passes, they begin to look at life through new lenses. The obstacles of indecision and difficulty with letting go, disappear. The two-thousand magazines they were going to read "someday" no longer feel important to keep. The thirty pairs of black pants are now easily reduced to five. The agony of deciding if things should stay or go suddenly disappears. Decisions become clearer, clutter is more easily released, and goals are achieved more quickly.

I am not suggesting that you turn your life upside-down to speed up the time it takes to accomplish things. I'm only pointing out that often after times of turmoil, the clarity people gain enables them to move forward at a changed pace.

Once the crisis passes, you begin to look at life through new lenses. The obstacles of indecision and difficulty with letting go, disappear. The two-thousand magazines you were going to read "someday" no longer feel important to keep.

TWO

Embrace Change

NORTON TRAVELS

We either EMBRACE CHANGE OR GO SCREAMING AND RUNNING AS FAST AS WE CAN IN THE OPPOSITE DIRECTION.

WHY IS IT THAT some of us fear change, while others seek it? Robert C. Gallagher gets to the heart of change in saying, "Change is inevitable—except from a vending machine." While that statement is both funny and true, we can't ignore the other piece, which has to do with attitudes about change. Our thoughts, both positive and negative, greatly affect how we perceive our lives. We can be encumbered or liberated by our ideas. Integral to change is our movement away from the familiar. For some, that thought will either be a frightening prospect or a thrilling opportunity.

Change Is Undeniable

While change is inevitable, the journey along the way can stir up deep emotions.

IT'S UNDENIABLE that change is upon us. Sometimes we seek it; sometimes it happens to us. The cold of winter conjured up a memory that marked a big change for my husband and me. We launched our oldest daughter, Allison, off to college. Simultaneously we began the cycle again to visit colleges with our younger daughter, Cassie. While these changes were expected, they still produced anxiety about the unknown and grief over losing the familiar. To help myself navigate these changes, I thought about how our girls view time. They look forward to the next step with anticipation, but without anxiety. They are focused on the current moment, do not brood about the past, and are ready to embrace the future. They are great reminders to me that while life changes, each stage has something wonderful to offer. As I encouraged myself to be in the present, my heart flooded with emotions as we shifted into a new phase of life.

Resisting Change

A small change today can deeply affect tomorrow.

HAVE YOU EVER NOTICED how difficult it is to change from the familiar to the unknown? The words "fear" and "resistance" come to mind, especially for people like me, who gravitate towards feeling secure and comfortable. I remember facing this type of challenge when I altered the way I organized my life.

I'd been using a conventional paper planner for ten years. It was an effective organizing tool for appointments, lists, addresses and thoughts. Over time, the pages became worn, and that disturbed my visual sensibility. Rewriting the pages would have been a time-consuming project, so I chose to investigate another option.

The winter signaled that a new year was about to begin. After much internal angst and debate, I decided to retire my paper planner and go electronic. This was a difficult decision because I was so attached to my traditional planner and couldn't imagine anything else working as effectively.

Thanks to the encouragement and expert advice from my husband Steve, who already owned a personal digital assistant (PDA), I moved forward into uncharted territory. Several evenings were spent at my computer entering appointments, addresses, and notes. This information was "hot-synched" to the PDA. To my amazement, within a week, I had completely switched over. The power and sophistication of the PDA far exceeded my paper planner's capabilities. I was surprised by how quickly I adapted once I made the decision to do so.

I recognize that my story is only about a planner. Many of you are confronting obstacles that are far more challenging. I encourage you to face them with gusto; the results will surprise you.

Navigating Change
Embracing change can help heal our hearts.

EACH SEASON BRINGS a transformation of scenery, weather, and another phase in my life. For many years, I collaborated on the *Norton*-inspired organizing cartoons with my good friend and artist, Richard Rockwell. I developed the concepts and initial sketches for the cartoons, while Richard turned my ideas into something beyond what I imagined. Norton was our family dog who passed away in 2005. In 2006, I had another loss when Richard passed away at age 85. In the winter of 2007, I published the last cartoon he drew for me.

I wanted to continue the series, but without Richard or Norton, I knew it was time to proactively seek change. I searched for another artist to collaborate on a new concept. After a long search, I found Mark Hill, a wonderful cartoonist. We spent months discussing concepts and working on sketches. That work eventually evolved into a new cartoon strip called "Super Pups." We produced several strips together and then discontinued them because the ideas had been exhausted.

Change has never been easy for me, especially when I haven't been ready to accept it. I missed both Richard and Norton. Despite my heartache, I allowed myself to be open to a new possibility. This enabled me to heal from my losses. When I published the new cartoons, I was able to appreciate the past and celebrate the present. I will always be grateful for Richard, Norton, Mark and the "Pups" for helping me negotiate the landscape of change.

Passion for Change

Some people are so passionate about change that they devote their lives to regularly seeking it in both small and big ways.

ON A RECENT WINTER DAY while sitting in my haircutter's chair, she matter-of-factly stated that she *loved* change. I was taken by surprise, since most people I know feel the exact opposite. I was curious about her statement and wanted to understand better. As I asked questions and listened, I was inspired by her spirit and with how she lives her life. I've thought about and shared this conversation with many others since then.

In what ways does she seek out change? She never takes the same route to work. On her days off, she never does the same thing. She regularly rearranges the furniture in her home. On a professional level, she tries different salons and haircutters every time she needs a haircut, to experience the way others do things. She incorporates what she likes and ignores the rest. The idea of routine is not part of her vocabulary. She thrives on change.

I was curious about her past. She moved many times while growing up. On the other hand, I lived in the same house from the time I was 18 months old until I left for college at 17. My parents still live in the house in which I grew up. I have only moved a few times in my life. I have to work hard to be flexible; my inclination towards familiarity was influenced deeply by my formative years.

People can have an assortment of reactions to their history. None of us respond in the same way. Even though I understand how I was influenced by my childhood and greatly appreciate the stability and love my parents gave me, I use that insight to help me push outside my comfort zone. Repeatedly my life lessons

If you fear change, try to recall past changes that had positive outcomes. Focus on those affirming experiences to help shift your attitude.

have taught me that through change comes tremendous growth. But since we don't own a crystal ball, we can't predict what that growth will be—and in the meantime, our fear can prevent us from venturing towards the unknown. I've learned to adapt to change and at other times to brazenly seek it out.

I am grateful to the words my haircutter shared. I get goosebumps when I think of her saying, "I *love* change!" Her words inspire me to go beyond where I'm comfortable, venture towards the unknown, and be a bit braver.

Change Is Everywhere
Let your past successes give you the confidence to grasp the change that you desire.

SOMETIMES CHANGE IS THRUST upon us. Sometimes we embrace it with open arms. Other times we try to prevent or resist it. Sometimes we proactively encourage things to transform. Often we've identified what we don't like about our current situation, but have difficulty envisioning what want we instead.

If you fear change, try to recall past changes that had positive outcomes. Focus on those affirming experiences to help shift your attitude. Years ago, when I thought about leaving the security of a job to start my own business, I was scared. At that time, our girls were babies. It felt risky to pursue a venture with many unknowns. I had endless conversations with my husband and father. After we crunched the numbers and agonized over the pros and cons, my dad said to me, "Go for it!" Those three words of confidence, which my dad was wise enough to utter, propelled me forward. I moved right past my fear and never looked back. It was one of the best decisions I ever made. I use that positive memory to keep propelling me ahead when doubt creeps in. I will be forever grateful to him for his enthusiastic encouragement.

Are all your choices supporting the changes you desire? Change occurs once we begin making different decisions. We may know what we want to achieve, but our choices don't always support our desired goal. Many people want a calm and clutter-free environment, but instead of releasing the piles of papers or overflowing closets of clothes, they struggle to do it.

Start by being aware that questions need to be asked. Be willing to challenge yourself. Continue to ask if your decisions will move you closer or farther away from the change you desire.

The road to change should be renamed www.bumpy-road.com (since everything these days seems to be a www.something.com). Going through change is rarely a straight or comfortable path. It is normal to experience ups and downs on your journey. You might find yourself taking a few steps forward and another few backwards. You want less chaos and clutter, and work hard to reduce it. You move ahead and gain control over areas of your life—and then will slip back a bit. You might be unreasonably hard on yourself. This up-and-down, forward-and-backward movement is a normal part of the experience. Move ahead anyway.

Readiness for Change

People change only when they are ready. They cannot be forced or cajoled.

ARE YOU ORGANIZATIONALLY challenged and ready for change? Knowing where you are on the path to greater organization will provide insight throughout your journey. On the path of change, some phases involve more thinking than actually doing, yet all are integral to the journey. Fluidity exists between the phases, and you'll sometimes feel yourself shifting forward and backwards between them. The process of change is not a direct route: It is more like a trip over hills and valleys.

I've identified five phases in the change process.

Phase 1 is *Initial Rumblings.* Before movement can occur, you will sense that something is bothering you. Has a book, article, TV show or talk with a friend raised some questions? Do you suspect that your disorganization has a negative effect on your daily life? If so, you are experiencing "initial rumblings" and are getting emotionally prepared for the next phase. You aren't ready to actually do anything yet, but you've identified your discomfort and have a heightened level of awareness. Some will remain here indefinitely; others will become restless and shift into the next phase.

Phase 2 is *Identifying Possibilities.* Before moving any further, you begin to ponder how to make change happen. You have identified your rumblings and are considering your options. You are becoming dissatisfied with how things are and desiring something different. You may feel anxious

The road to change should be renamed www.bumpyroad.com since everything these days seems to be a www.something.com. Going through change is rarely a straight or comfortable path.

and paralyzed to make changes by yourself and consider enlisting outside help. In this phase, you might start thinking about hiring a professional organizer. The key here is *thinking about*. Perhaps you still aren't fully committed to changing. You might feel apprehensive about verbalizing your thoughts and asking for help.

Phase 3 is *Reaching Out*. The feelings of pain and being overwhelmed have increased to the point where you cautiously take another step. Instead of just thinking about change, you pick up the phone or send an e-mail to a professional organizer, therapist, family member or friend. You acknowledge that you cannot accomplish your desired changes alone. After interviewing several organizers, you are hopeful that change is possible with the right kind of support. You might remain here for a while until your commitment level increases and you shift into the next phase.

Phase 4 is *Beyond Talking*. You have contemplated, researched, and become ready for action. In this phase, you are feeling determined and ready to devote the physical, emotional, and financial resources necessary for making changes. You've hired a professional organizer and are starting to work on your organizing challenges. You may feel relieved because someone is helping you, and simultaneously impatient because "the work" is more difficult than you anticipated. While you are committed to moving forward and feel positive, the progress may be slow. You might remain in Phase 4 for a long time as you experience the ups and downs of the change process.

Phase 5 is *Life Jolts*. Circumstances can occur which transform your outlook and commitment level. Major life events such as death of a loved one, divorce, illness, changes in medication, new job, or children leaving the nest can affect the organizing process positively or negatively. When the reaction is positive, these types of events can alter your perspective significantly, which can in turn bring about quick and decisive changes. You become clearer than ever about what you want. You no longer struggle with what to keep or release. You have a sense of clarity that you have not previously experienced. Progress quickens. You are energized.

When people are ready, they change. Their initiative and desire must come from within. When the pain to stay the same becomes greater than the fear of the unknown, change occurs. As Anais Nin said, "There came a time when the risk to remain tight in the bud was more painful than the risk it took to blossom." Change is possible with desire, determination, commitment and a compassionate support system.[1]

---

1   Linda Samuels wrote *Readiness of Change* for the NSGCD (National Study Group on Chronic Disorganization.) That version is available through www.nsgcd.org under Fact Sheets.

When people are ready,
they change.

THREE

Next Step

NORTON PRIORITIZES

Being clear ABOUT YOUR GOALS AND PRIORITIES WILL MAKE THE NEXT STEP EASIER TO TAKE.

UNTIL YOU DETERMINE what you are trying to accomplish, it will be difficult to identify what comes next. Sometimes the end goal seems so far away that we intimidate ourselves into inaction. Keep your vision in mind, but don't let your thoughts race too far ahead. Just take one step, then another, then one more. As Lao Tzu said, "A journey of a thousand miles begins with but a single step."

The Mind Diet
Record the floating lists from your brain and then move forward.

IT AMAZES ME how much mental energy it takes to *think* about the things on our to-do lists. When we finally decide to act on what we've been pondering, it feels great and doesn't seem so intimidating. The results can be spectacular. It's like going on a *mind diet*. By doing what we've been thinking about, we reduce our stress and anxiety. We release our minds from thousands of stray thoughts. This process can energize us.

Somehow the anguish we put ourselves through—thinking about how we'll do it, when we'll do it, or how long it will take to complete, can overpower us into inactivity. I often see this with clients. What feels overwhelming becomes manageable once we take the first step together. Perhaps your challenge is organizing decades of photos, or perhaps tackling the overflowing closets or rooms full of kids' toys. If you find yourself mulling over the list too often, that's your cue. It's time to start. Dig in. Take action. If it still seems impossible, enlist the help of a friend or professional organizer to work with you.

No goal can be reached without action. Pick your project. Refer to your goals list. Then take the next step.

Beyond Chaos
Release the things beyond your control and focus on the things you can do something about.

IN THIS TIME OF CHAOS and uncertainty, feeling organized can be essential to our well-being. We have very little control over many things in life. Surprises seem to usurp our plans along the way. When we take control over particular areas of our life, we create a certain amount of internal peace and calm. As the world around us seems to be spinning out of control, we can stop to ask ourselves, "What can I do to improve my daily routine or environment?" We can't solve the global economic crisis, but we can find ways to clear our physical and mental clutter. I encourage you to take control over the things you can change.

Organizing Mood

Organizing will be much easier if you establish the optimal conditions for working.

WHEN YOU ARE READY to begin the organizing process, make sure you create the right mood to enhance success. We are all prone to distractions. Common interruptions are ringing phones, doorbells, e-mails, children, pets, or internal thoughts. Think about how you can carve out a chunk of organizing time and eliminate some of your distractions. Figure out ways to minimize yours. You know best what pulls you away from your tasks.

To set the right tone for organizing, some find that it helps to listen to music while they work. Some like to sing or hum along. Notice if the music enhances or hinders the process. Experiment with different types of music along with the volume to determine which are the optimal working parameters. Alternatively, some may concentrate better if there is complete silence.

Establish a set amount of time to organize. Since taking the next step can be intimidating, making an agreement with yourself to only work for a specific time can greatly improve your chances of moving ahead. Use a timer to help you stay on track, structure work sessions and focus your effort. What amount of time works best for you? Can you focus for 15 or 30 minutes at a stretch, or do you prefer longer sessions? Let the timer assist you.

Decide in advance what you want to accomplish during your organizing time. It's easy to just jump in, but some planning will help direct your work efforts. At the beginning of every organizing session with my clients, we take time to discuss what we want to accomplish for that visit. The discussion helps to refocus goals and stay on track.

Most importantly, to create the right mood for organizing, make sure you're sending the "I can do it" message to your brain. It's common to be negative and make excuses for postponing action, and I've heard many people berate themselves. Fight the temptation to be negative. Psych yourself up to be positive. Move forward.

Preparation
To move ahead with your organizing efforts, take time to prepare.

YOUR POSSESSIONS TAKE both physical and emotional space. It is possible that you have too much stuff. If so, admitting this fact is an important part of preparing for action. Are your possessions making it difficult for you to live the life you desire? While they can literally crowd our spaces, the distress and energy we use to think about them can also take an emotional toll on our well-being. We can spend so much time thinking about and moving our stuff around that our things begin to direct us rather than the other way around. Those feelings can lead to unconscious stress and anxiety.

If you are ready to begin the editing process, make sure you put on your "ruthless cap." Adopting that attitude will help you make more deliberate choices about your possessions. Give yourself permission to both let go of things that you no longer want and keep the items that are meaningful. If you are having difficulty making decisions, consider bringing in an organizing buddy for help. Enlisting the right support can often simplify the decision-making process.

It is possible that you have too much stuff. If so, admitting this fact is an important part of preparing for action.

Daily To-Do List
Don't underestimate the power of the to-do list.

IS YOUR LONG TO-DO LIST floating around in your brain or have you committed it to paper? Writing down your lists will clear your mind of clutter, help consolidate your thoughts, and enable you to select your next action.

Regarding lists, there are many ways to make them. Some like to write on scraps of paper or sticky notes. Others like to use pads. Sometimes people prefer to record their lists on answering machines or other electronic devices. Some use a combination of list-making techniques to keep them on track. What type of list will work best for you?

Here is one method to think about. Date your list. Consider grouping similar items together like "To-Do," "Calls to Make" and "Errands." Your efficiency will increase when you handle similar items at the same time. Keep your list flexible. Add and delete items as needed. When your list becomes too difficult to read, take the time to redo it. Carry over only unfinished items to the new list.

Be aware of your top one or two daily priorities. Ask yourself, "If I accomplished only one item today, which one is most important?" After that item is complete, select the next most important item. Begin and end your day by reviewing your list. This will help you shape your day and keep you focused.

Master List

Use your "Master List" to capture long-term and lower-priority projects and goals.

THERE ARE MANY TYPES of lists. Some are short-term, while others are long-term. The Master List gives you the ability to capture those far-reaching and larger goals that cannot be done quickly or in one step. The Master List acts as a placeholder to record your ideas and revisit them later.

Keeping separate, ongoing Master Lists for various areas of your life can be an effective organizing tool. These lists will most likely include long-term and non-urgent items that do not yet have specific deadlines. They are items that you don't want to forget, but you are not yet ready to schedule. Some examples of a Master Lists include "Master List, Personal" or "Master List, Business." The personal list might have items like "Organize photos," "Revamp filing system," or "Organize the basement." The business list might include items such as "Write a presentation," "Update Website," or "Organize contacts." Review Master Lists weekly. Incorporate items onto your daily lists as appropriate by breaking down the larger projects into smaller tasks.

*Writing down your lists will clear
your mind of clutter, help consolidate
your thoughts, and enable you to
select your next action step.*

Moving Forward

Stepping back to see an overview of the organizing process is useful in figuring out what comes next.

I RECOGNIZE THAT FOR SOME, organizing alone might be impossible. It might be beneficial to find a guide to help with this journey. An overview will be your roadmap in the organizing process.

First, determine if you are ready to devote time to the process. Do not let your past failures discourage you from the possibility of future success. Do everything necessary to make the conditions right for change.

Whether you try this on your own or with assistance, here is one plan for negotiating the organizing process. Establish your priorities and goals. From there, use your list-making skills to determine which potential projects you want to work on. Select the project you want to begin with. Break the project down into small, manageable parts. Schedule time so that you use both small and large blocks of time. Stay with the project from start to finish, understanding that there will be distractions and life challenges along the way that can pull you off course. Just recognize that challenges are an integral, normal part of the process. The key is coming back even after you've been sidetracked. Continue until your project has been completed. Return to your list to select the next project. Repeat the process.

We do not know what our challenges will be. We can only prepare emotionally for the fact that we will have them. As Frank Clark said, "If you can find a path with no obstacles, it probably doesn't lead anywhere."

II

Spring

"What the world really needs is more love and less paperwork."
—PEARL BAILEY

SPRING IS A TIME FOR RENEWAL. AS THE AIR BECOMES WARMER, A NEW SENSE OF HOPE AND JOY SURROUNDS ME. I NOTICE THE MOIST SMELL OF THE EARTH, THE MAGICAL SIGHT OF FOLIAGE REAPPEARING, AND THE FEAST OF FLOWER BUDS OPENING, WHICH RETURNS COLOR TO THE SEASON. MY HEART FEELS LIGHTER AS I SLOW DOWN, AND AM INSPIRED BY THE TRANSFORMATION BEFORE ME.

FOUR

Too Hard to Let Go

NORTON CHOOSES

Sometimes we have TO BE BRAVE ENOUGH TO LET GO IN ORDER TO CREATE ROOM FOR NEW POSSIBILITIES.

WHY IS IT SO HARD to let go? We hold on to our possessions, our busy schedules, and our familiar routines. Do we think that if we let go, we will lose a part of who we are? We can potentially hold on so tightly that we deny ourselves the joy felt from releasing, making space for something wonderful, and experiencing tremendous growth.

Release and Blossom

It is incredibly liberating when you give yourself permission to let go.

IT TAKES AN ENORMOUS amount of emotional energy
to "hold on." When you let go, you make room for positive
thoughts and create an environment for growth. You discover
that life can be just fine without your micromanagement of
everyone and everything.

One spring when Allison was 17, she began talking about
volunteering in Thailand to teach English. At first, the idea of
her traveling to the other side of the world by herself was frightening to Steve and me. After much deliberation, I realized that
I didn't want my fears to get in the way of her confidence. As
she prepared to leave, I focused on relinquishing my worries. In
the process, there was a blossoming all around. She had a life-
changing, confidence-building experience and I learned that
only by letting go could wings spread and growth occur.

As you face your challenge, whether it's papers, possessions, growing children, or other issues, remember that you
can develop in ways never imagined when you allow yourself
to let go.

It takes an enormous amount of emotional energy to "hold on." When you let go, you make room for positive thoughts and create an environment for growth.

One Box
Our personal history influences the decisions we make.

AS SPRING UNFOLDED, I felt the need to cull our overflowing collection of books. I posed the same questions I often ask clients. "Do you *really* want this book?" "Has it served its purpose?" "Has it overstayed its welcome?" "Is the dust on the cover an indicator of how recently this book was read?"

My goal was to donate many boxes of books to our local library so that I could liberate some shelf space for other books. However, after several hours of reviewing our collection, I only managed to release one box. I had difficulty parting with much of our collection and experienced the dilemma that many of my clients face. After all, books don't go bad. Even though I hadn't necessarily looked at them recently, I *might* want to. They were still very interesting and potentially useful. In addition, some of our collection belonged to my husband and he wasn't ready to part with many. Why was I having so much difficulty letting go?

I began thinking about the family I came from and our attitudes toward books. Growing up, while on family outings, we often ended up in a bookstore, "Just to browse." As a family, we'd spend hours looking, reading, and sometimes purchasing books. My parents traveled the world. They bought books to prepare for their journeys and brought new ones home to share where they'd been. Their coffee table continues to host a changing collection on topics ranging from art, music, technology, humor, and more. Their bedside tables are always stacked high with titles they are reading now or next. Every room in their house has books, organized by categories.

Books were welcome and coveted gifts for birthdays and other special occasions. My brother and sister never went anywhere without something to read. My family simply loves books and their passion was passed on to me. As a result, our house is full of them.

As I attempted to part with my collection, I thought about the influences from my past. I felt grateful for the forward movement I had taken. That day I only ended up releasing one box of books from our household library, but I gained a new appreciation of the struggle many of my clients experience between the pull of keeping and letting go.

Emotional Time Travel

Organizing and touching our possessions can conjure up memories from our past. Releasing them can create space for our present.

SEVERAL SPRINGS AGO, a few people shared experiences about organizing and I discovered some interesting common feelings. Each person talked about how it felt to go through closets overflowing with clothes, papers bursting from file drawers, or basements filled with things they didn't know they had. In every instance, it was difficult to make decisions about what to keep and what to release. Despite challenges, each person worked through them because they felt *compelled* to let go. They had come to the point where they "just *had* to." They were ready to part with the past to make space for the present and future.

People shared with me that going through their possessions was like visiting a former self. They came upon clothes that had not been seen or worn for decades. Upon finding "those pants" or other items from another phase in their

Sometimes our possessions hold us back and we don't realize this until we're ready to let go and experience what life feels like without them.

life, the organizing process felt like emotional time travel for them. The found object enabled them to reflect about that other time, recognize that it was in the past and that they had moved on. They wondered why they still owned the object. This process enabled them to release the physical object while honoring its memory.

After letting go of those objects, they each experienced a great sense of accomplishment and relief. One woman said she felt as if she'd "just lost 30 pounds!" Another said that it felt as if a great weight had been lifted. Sometimes our possessions hold us back and we don't realize this until we're ready to let go and experience what life feels like without them. When we allow ourselves to question our reasons for holding on, this can enable us to let go. We open our lives to possibilities and feelings we couldn't have anticipated.

Birth Day

Becoming a parent marks another kind of letting go.

BOTH OF OUR DAUGHTERS were born in the spring. When Allison arrived, I experienced my first "letting go" parenting lesson. While pregnant, I carried her wherever I went. When she was born, the cord was cut and she was moved twenty feet away from me for observation. While we were elated that Allison had finally arrived, my heart ached because they had physically taken her away from me. It was the first time we were separated. My emotions were the strangest combination of joy and pain—and this was just my first in a long line of "letting go" parenting lessons.

At many points along the way, Steve and I either intuitively knew to let go or we were *encouraged* by our daughters that "it was time." At each juncture, we learned to let them do things themselves, give them room to explore, and make mistakes along with great discoveries. If we hovered too much, we knew we'd hinder their growth and self-confidence. Of course, this was not always easy to do. The instinct to protect your children at all costs is very intense. It's much harder to watch your children experience pain or frustration. However, you cannot learn their life lessons for them.

It's a delicate balance between guiding and stepping back. The letting go lessons of parenting translate into other challenges such as letting go of possessions that overwhelm us. Each of us can benefit from releasing the things that hold us back so that we can make space for growth.

Letting Go

We have difficultly letting go for many reasons, especially when our possessions hold sentimental value.

IT'S DIFFICULT TO IMAGINE our lives without our special possessions. We all own treasures that remind us of our past or the people we love. It's normal to want to keep things. But consider being selective about what you keep. Take photos or write about your possessions and their significance. Once you've done that, give or donate the actual pieces to people that will value them. You can safely release the physical objects and still honor their memory.

Another reason we keep things is because they are familiar and comfortable. We create a "nest" of objects that surround us. We recognize them as ours and find comfort in their existence. Even if they have outlived their purpose or usefulness, we are accustomed to their presence. Familiarity alone is not in itself a reason to hold on. If these things are taking up space and they are no longer needed, consider releasing them.

We don't always take time to ask questions about our possessions. Things enter our lives, are barely used and gather dust. It sometimes seems easier to let things accumulate than to take the time to evaluate if they are adding value to our lives. So we collect, pile and stack. Our spaces become overrun by objects and papers before we realize what is happening. Ask yourself, "Have they overstayed their welcome?" If so, let your things move on.

We keep things because we *might* need them someday. This perhaps is one of the most common reasons I hear from clients. This can happen with papers, books, kitchenware, clothes, assorted cords, electronic devices and more. The items in question haven't been looked at or used for years, but the feeling exists that at some point they might be useful. It's the caveat of *might* that prevents us from letting go. The need for the objects may never arrive. Instead, the items end up cluttering both your mind and your space.

Incentive to Let Go
If you no longer use it, release it.

THE LESS YOU HAVE, the easier it is to stay organized. If you are struggling with letting go, think about what will help you move on. If you want to get organized, a first step involves editing and releasing the excess.

You will not be able to organize effectively until you've decided what is essential to keep or pass on. How much time do you spend managing your things rather than using them? Are you living your life doing what is meaningful or has the care of your possessions taken top priority? There is nothing wrong with owning things, but are they controlling your life? How many things do you really want or need? Can someone else benefit from them? Can you donate to a charity or give to a friend? It can be very satisfying to pass along the items you no longer use. By doing so, they get a new life, a chance to be appreciated by someone else and an opportunity for you to make space in your life for what's important.

The Future

There is a delicate balance between respecting our history and making room for the future.

IN KARA SWANSON'S BOOK, *I'll Carry the Fork*, she wrote, "I learned the hard way that as long as you stay in the past, you cannot have a future. No matter how hard it is you have to let go." Our attitudes and possessions can hold us back. We can never fully separate from our past because it is our history that makes us who we are. It's just that if we define our lives only by our past, we block the potential for what might lay ahead. If you are struggling with holding on to something—whether it's an attitude or an object—give yourself the opportunity to let go and see how it influences your feelings about the future.

Are you living your life doing what is meaningful or has the care of your possessions taken top priority? There is nothing wrong with owning things, but are they controlling your life?

FIVE

Too Much Clutter

NORTON ORGANIZES

People have unique PERCEPTIONS OF THAT CROSSOVER POINT WHEN POSSESSIONS BECOME CLUTTER.

CLUTTER CAN BE SEEN in many ways. In extreme cases, our possessions can accumulate to the point where it becomes impossible to function. While our perception of clutter varies, the common theme is that our possessions prevent us from living the lives we envision.

The Extremes of Clutter
Clutter is in the eyes of the beholder.

ONE OF THE MOST fascinating things I've learned from clients is that the definition of clutter depends upon the lens through which you look. It is our perception more than any other factor that defines clutter and our relationship to it. There are several good sources for describing what clutter looks like. The National Study Group on Chronic Disorganization developed the NSGCD Clutter Hoarding Scale as "an assessment measurement tool to give professional organizers and related professionals definitive parameters."[1] Drs. Randy Frost and Gail Steketee developed the Clutter Image Rating Scale, which is a visual, photographic tool for identifying the viewer's perception of clutter levels within specific rooms.[2]

These tools are great reference points, but they do not reveal the entire story. I have been surprised more than once to discover that one person's organizing starting point is another person's end goal. In the initial calls I receive from potential clients, I often hear the same words: "I am *overwhelmed* with my disorganization and clutter." While during our call I take time to learn about their situation, I know that until I actually see what they are describing, I won't fully understand the situation. I've also noticed that their perception and circumstance colors what they are describing. Often there are discrepancies between what they describe and what I actually observe when I visit.

---

1 The NSGCD Clutter Hoarding Scale is available through www.nsgcd.org.
2 The Clutter Image Rating Scale is included in the *Compulsive Hoarding and Acquiring* workbook by Drs. Gail Steketee and Randy Frost, published by Oxford University Press, 2007.

One spring early on in my organizing career, I received a call from a potential client who was distressed. She was completely overwhelmed by her clutter and wasn't sure that anybody could help. She could barely think because there was "so much visual noise and clutter in her home." At our first meeting, we sat in her living room to get to know one another and discuss her goals. I didn't see any clutter and thought perhaps this was the "clutter-free room." As we talked, she apologized multiple times for the chaos in the living room. I thought about *The Emperor's New Clothes*, because the clutter wasn't visible to me. I felt a bit awkward, but finally asked her to show me the clutter. She pointed out a small pile of books on an end table to indicate the clutter. Then she explained that the "worst clutter" was on her desk and in her closet but that she was embarrassed to show me. At this point, I assumed that the main issues were in these other rooms and respected that she needed more time to feel comfortable with me before sharing this part of her home. After we talked some more, I asked if she was ready to let me see the other areas. When she showed me, I was even more confused. On her desk were about four pieces of paper. In her closet were only a few shirts and pants, maybe ten items at the most. She became visibly distressed as she talked about the volume of clutter on her desk and in her closet.

This was an interesting challenge. She was overwhelmed by her physical possessions, but from my perspective, there were hardly any objects to work with. As we talked more, I realized that her clutter tolerance level was extremely low. In addition, her lack of confidence when making decisions overwhelmed her. I began asking questions about her vision for how she wanted her desk and closet to be. She reiterated that she wanted "less clutter and clearer spaces." We began with the desk. I asked about each piece of paper. We discussed its significance and if it was in the right place. It took her a long time to evaluate and make decisions, but together we were able to organize things in a way that satisfied her. We worked together many times after that. Each time she shared how much better she felt at the end of our visits. She could "think and breathe better."

Around the same time, I received another call from a potential client. He described that he had so much clutter he was unable to sleep in his bedroom or cook in his kitchen. The thought of anyone entering his home would cause his heart to palpitate because he was petrified to let anyone see how he was living. He had gone through a severe depression, during which he stopped taking care of his physical environment. After many years, the depression lifted and he felt completely over-whelmed with the condition of his home. During his depression, he didn't notice the clutter, but after the fog lifted, he saw it clearly and couldn't figure out how to move ahead.

When I first arrived, I could barely walk in. Unlike the client I described before, this client's clutter *was* visible. He had accurately described his situation. We continued working together regularly for many years until his home reflected his vision.

What I've described are two extremes of my experience as an organizer. Most of my experiences have fallen somewhere in between. I feel honored to be invited into so many lives, and am grateful for the lessons clients have taught me about perception, patience and perseverance.

One of the most fascinating things J've learned from clients is that the definition of clutter depends upon the lens through which you look. Jt is our perception more than any other factor that defines clutter and our relationship to it.

Taming the Clutter
If your possessions are overwhelming you, activate your editing options.

IT'S TIME TO CONFESS. Our two-car garage was the place things entered but rarely left. While "garage" was its official name, it housed everything but cars. Our garage became the storage area for our house, which has no attic or basement. Even though my husband had organized the garage several times before, it had once again gotten out of control.

Inspired by our need to create an area for his drums, we were determined to improve the situation. Spring seemed like the ideal time to work on this project. We edited, organized, and rethought the space. Being clear about our goal made the process much easier. We released things that we no longer wanted. It was energizing to create piles of discards outside and workable space inside. We felt a sense of accomplishment as we tamed the space. For weeks after we organized, I kept going to "just look" at the work we'd done. Instead of feeling embarrassed about the space, I felt proud and elated.

We all have our own "garages" in life. Sometimes they need to be revisited more than once. I encourage you to identify yours and make the time to face it head on.

Clutter Tolerance
We each have different clutter tolerance levels.

WE PERCEIVE AND DEFINE clutter differently. If you live on your own, then your clutter issues only affect you. What happens, though, when you live or work with other people whose views about clutter are vastly different from yours? It is challenging enough just to work on your own issues, but when you factor other people into the mix, the situation becomes complex.

If you have a challenge with clutter, is it just your issue or is your clutter affecting people that you live or work with? Perhaps your clutter isn't a problem for you, but your spouse, parent, child or boss is finding it problematic. What do you do? There is no one answer because situations vary greatly. One thing to keep in mind is that once other people are involved, you're not in this alone. You'll want to think about not just your relationship to clutter but also how it affects others.

One possible way to think about this is to create "personal areas" where you can express yourself any way you like. Establish "communal areas" where everyone's preferences are considered and negotiated. In our home, we all have different levels of comfort regarding clutter. I tend to like the least amount and Allison tends to like the most. She finds comfort in the visual stimulation of her physical possessions surrounding her. I also enjoy looking at my "toys" or photos, but prefer to have things displayed rather than piled around me. Cassie and Steve are somewhere in between our extremes. Our house is small with a lot of communal areas, so while not always successful, we try to work together to respect each other's clutter preferences as best as possible.

Experiences instead of Things
There are gift-giving alternatives that can reduce clutter and increase positive memories.

OUR DAUGHTERS CERTAINLY had their share of toys, but often they invented their own games and fun. Celebrating birthdays and special events along with gift-giving was integral to their childhoods. Over time, however, it became increasingly difficult to find the right gift because neither of them, especially Cassie, wanted more "things."

When Cassie was quite young, we asked her what she would like for one of her birthdays. She asked if we could "give her experiences instead of things." Cassie's question helped reframe our view about gifts. We changed our focus from *giving* things to *doing* things. We substituted clothing, jewelry and toys for plays, special days, and adventures. It's been interesting to replace giving "stuff" with instead giving opportunities for more time together. We've received the benefit of minimizing clutter and filling our hearts with wonderful memories.

Clutter gathers because our possessions accumulate, get relegated to piles, corners, closets or drawers and then get ignored. The editing process has not occurred.

Managing Clutter
Less is easier to organize and maintain.

DO YOUR PAPERS and possessions overwhelm you? There are several methods that may help you reduce your clutter.

Clutter gathers because our possessions accumulate, get relegated to piles, corners, closets or drawers and then get ignored. The editing process has *not* occurred. After deciding that you want less clutter, start asking questions about your stuff. One of my favorites is, "Has it overstayed its welcome?" We often hang on to things long past their usefulness for that "someday" which never comes. It might be time to say goodbye to those things that are causing clutter and no longer benefiting you.

Sometimes we feel we "*have* to" be the collector of all the information. This feeling comes up often when I'm sorting paper with clients. Ask yourself, "Do I have to be the keeper of the paper? If I released it and were to need it, could I get it again?" These simple questions might enable you to part with more and keep less. Some are fearful to let go of papers, even nonessential ones, even if they could easily be acquired again *if* they were needed in the future. But consider the 80/20 rule when questioning. For example, we only use 20 percent of the papers we file, clothes we own or toys our kids have. The remaining 80 percent is never used! That 80 percent is probably the root cause of most of your clutter.

Paper Clutter

Someone once stated that we'd have a paperless society when we have a paperless toilet.

ALMOST A DECADE AGO, the paperless toilet arrived, yet unlike the prediction, we still are far from living in a paperless society. In fact, we seem to have more paper than ever. If you are struggling with your piles, you are not alone. While people face a variety of organizational challenges in the digital age, the most common one is pervasive paper clutter.

Let's be honest about our papers. If your piles are too high and your filing cabinets so full that you can't easily find the documents you need, you might consider making some changes.

Many people despise looking at their piles, let alone touching them. By postponing the work, are you making the task more difficult? One way to get through your papers is to set a timer for 15 minutes, crank up the music, and play the "Sort and Release" game. When the timer rings, stop working. Instead of having a marathon session and facing potential burnout, try to work in regular, short, focused intervals.

If the growing piles of paper are causing you more distress than the effort involved in organizing, and you are finding it impossible to sort papers on your own, you are one among many. I encourage you to enlist help from a friend, family member, or professional.

Clothing Clutter
If one is enough, why have two?

ARE YOUR CLOSETS and drawers overflowing with clothing? Do your clothes need more space to breathe? Do you want to make getting dressed easier? Think about what your closet looks like now and how it is or isn't functioning. Here are some ideas to help you transform your closet, reduce your clothing clutter and help you feel more in control.

First, consider if it will be easier to organize your clothes with the help of a friend, family member or professional. If so, don't hesitate to enlist their assistance in advance. Organizing clothes is a physical process, and an extra pair of hands is often welcome. It's also useful to have a second and objective opinion when trying on clothes.

Prepare by setting up large bags or boxes labeled "Donate," "Resale," "Discard," "Launder/Repair," and "Maybe." Your helper can place items into the correct piles as you make decisions. If you aren't sure which pile to relegate something to, place it in the "Maybe" pile. Just be careful that you don't let too many items end up with the "Maybes." The idea is to decide now and not postpone the decision-making. But if a particular item is causing difficulties, it's better to put it aside and move on to the next item, rather than letting it slow down your editing process.

Begin with one drawer or closet section at a time and repeat until you've gone through all areas. Systematically evaluate one clothing item at a time. Release items that you no longer wear, that no longer fit or that are beyond repair. Keep only items you love, flatter you, and are appropriate for your lifestyle. If you need additional space for your clothes after you've edited them, remove out-of-season and sentimental clothing. Store them in an alternate location such as in an under-the-bed storage container or in another closet.

Once you've completed editing, it's time to think about how you want to organize your clothes. There is no right or wrong way. It's a matter of figuring out what works best for you and how you process. Many people prefer to arrange similar things together (pants with pants, skirts with skirts and short sleeves with short sleeves.) Others prefer to hang outfits together. Some like to group clothes according to type, such as work, casual and dressy. Some prefer to group by color, while others are not concerned about the color order. Your objective is to organize in a way that works best for you.

We often hang on to things long past their usefulness for that "someday" which never comes.

Minimizing Clutter

You will have better clutter management if you take the time to establish "homes" for your things.

CLUTTER ACCUMULATES for many reasons. The most frequent reason I've observed has to do with objects that lack a home. Sometimes this occurs because there is not enough space for your things. While this is a significant issue, and requires editing and releasing to solve, the other issue is that sometimes we just haven't made a decision about where our things should go.

For example, how many times have you misplaced your keys? I have an unreasonable fear of losing my car and house keys. This fear drives me to be a bit obsessive about them. I refuse to let them out of my hand until I place them in their designated spot in my purse. The key word here is "designated."

How do you determine where your things should go? The goal is to place things closest to where you will need them. For example, it makes sense that items you use in the kitchen should be located there. It's not just a matter of putting kitchen items in that room, but also thinking about how you move through and use the space. Cooking utensils might be most useful near the stove. Coffee mugs might be stored in a cabinet near the coffeemaker. You can think about creating stations in the kitchen for the different types of things you do. The overriding idea is to give every object, from the smallest tool to the largest pot, a strategic place to call home.

The other trick is to return the objects to their home, which is integral to maintaining the systems you've established. You can spend a lot of time organizing and finding places for all your things. To make this effective, however, you will also need to put the objects back in their places when you finish with them. I call this *full-circle thinking.* If you open a drawer, close it. If you use a pot, wash it and put it back in the cabinet where it came from.

The reality is that you may not be able to constantly put things away; that might make you feel a bit frenetic. However, you can give yourself stopping points during the day or week to clear the decks and get things back to square one. For some, especially nonlinear thinkers, the maintenance part is a challenge—so they might want to consider enlisting help from others.

Supportive Environment

You will be amazed at how much less stress you'll have when your environment is organized to support you.

ONE SPRING, when our family went on vacation, we rented a house that was extremely organized. Everything was labeled, from light switches to kitchen drawers to cabinet shelves. I derived a certain comfort in knowing where the spoons or dishtowels went. I didn't have to search or spend mental energy guessing where things were. While I wouldn't necessarily want my own home labeled as such, I loved the idea of everything having a specific place. Here we were in a house we didn't know and we could easily find and put away everything. It set the mood for a simple, stress-free vacation.

When you think about your environment, do you struggle to locate things or can you easily find what you need? If you are hunting often, a worthwhile goal might be to release everything that is extraneous and establish homes for all that remains.

Not Later, But Now!
Use the "Do now!" concept to avoid clutter.

AS NEW THINGS ENTER YOUR HOME, whether it's mail, groceries, gifts or dry cleaning, test the "Do now!" concept by putting them away immediately. That way, they won't collect in piles and corners. This practice also encourages us to be conscious of what is coming in and where it needs to go.

Does it always work? We are human, so of course it won't always happen. But the idea is that if we do this as frequently as possible, we will create less work for later. Once piles begin to collect, the task to organize, route things and make decisions becomes larger. Adopting the "Do now!" concept minimizes the amount of time and effort spent managing the stuff of life.

This idea might not be so easy for those that tend to procrastinate, especially when it comes to mundane tasks such as sorting mail. For procrastinators, building in excitement and activating some adrenaline might make this technique work more successfully. One method might be to set a timer and play "Beat the Clock" by attempting to put things away *before* the buzzer goes off.

Once piles begin to collect, the task to organize, route things and make decisions becomes larger. Adopting the "Do now!" concept minimizes the amount of time and effort spent managing the stuff of life.

SIX

Too Little Time

NORTON SCHEDULES

The goal of effective time management ISN'T TO CRAM MORE THINGS INTO YOUR 24 HOURS, BUT TO HELP YOU FOCUS ON WHAT'S IMPORTANT.

EACH DAY IS A GIFT, and it gives us the opportunity to figure out how we want to use our time. There is no question that life is busy. Sometimes it seems as if we have no direction for our days. There are ways to rethink the schedule to make it more the way you envision. While we do not have total control, we do have choices and the ability to be selective.

The "Y" Word

Choose your yeses carefully to avoid being overscheduled.

THERE'S SOMETHING SPECIAL about spring. The weather is warmer, clothes are lighter, and flowers are peeking through the earth. One can see, hear, feel and smell the changes as winter departs and spring emerges. Spring is a particularly busy time for me. Normally I choose my commitments very carefully, making sure I don't say yes to more than I can handle. Somehow, though, in my zest for the new, one spring in particular, I said the "y" word too many times and found myself more stressed than usual.

So what tricks did I use to keep sane and organized? I made lists and got a reasonable amount of sleep instead of staying up too late. I reviewed and prepared for the next day the night before and relied on my PDA to manage my to-dos, time and contacts. I reminded myself to be flexible and I tried to do only one thing at a time. I remained present, focusing on what I was doing and where I was at that moment. I leaned on family and friends for emotional support.

Just as spring brings new growth, new items will appear on my list. As one list gets completed, another one emerges. The lists are like the seasons—one flowing into the next. My objective is to learn from the challenges and to be grateful for each moment.

Perfect Day
Make time to enjoy those perfect days.

LIFE ISN'T JUST ABOUT preparing, planning and organizing. It's also about having the time to experience wonderful days. While all the seasons are unique, spring holds a special place in my heart. It's impossible to feel bad when the heavy clothes of winter are shed for jacket-free weather, the sun shines brightly, birds are singing, the air smells sweet with new growth and the landscape shifts from monotone to Technicolor.

One early spring day, I went with my family to a park along the Hudson River. Steve was playing in a Zydeco band that afternoon. Cassie and I went to hear him. People of all ages were out with their chairs and picnic blankets to enjoy the day, the music and one another. One of our friends brought dozens of giant hula-hoops for everyone to use. It was a wonderful mix of people, music, and dancing by the river. As the day turned into night, the fireworks began. Together we watched as the sky lit up with an amazing display of colors. I felt grateful for being part of this perfect spring day.

Life isn't just about preparing, planning and organizing. It's also about having the time to experience wonderful days.

Making Choices

Our choices can either overwhelm us or make us feel more in control of our time.

DO YOU FEEL OVERWHELMED when you have no time to relax? Consider some of the following questions and how you might alter your current schedule to feel less stressed.

How many nights a week are you out? Each person has his or her own threshold of becoming overwhelmed. I find that if I am away more than a few times a week, I feel overwhelmed. It's worth testing out your threshold by making adjustments in your schedule, and noting how your feel.

Does going out in the evenings prevent you from having time to unwind and handle basic responsibilities? It doesn't work well for me when I don't have enough time for the basics, because running in too many directions overwhelms me. Frustration sets in when I'm unable to accomplish tasks that need my attention.

Do you eat dinner together as a family, or is everyone going in a different direction? There is nothing like having meals together to reconnect and relax. I'll admit that there are times when we are unsuccessful at this, but committing to even one night a week together makes a big difference in the quality of our time.

Do you have any unscheduled time in your week to do whatever you wish? Do you have any free weekends or are they completely filled with activities? Sometimes we plan so much that we forget to take time to just float. I am a planner and often know my schedule months in advance. I also make sure there is unscheduled time in my calendar. Having time available for doing something or nothing helps me create more balance in my life.

Are you living in an emergency mode? The stress can be taxing on the mind and body. Sometimes these crises are impossible to control. Since they do take a toll, it's important to look at other ways to balance your time so that you can replenish the energy that the emergencies consume. This might mean letting go of other obligations, making time for self-care, or taking a break and getting away even if it's just for a day.

Do you have difficulty saying no? Why is that? Is it that we like to be the "go-to" person? Is it that we don't want to disappoint people? Is it that we feel obligated to say yes? Take a good look at your reasons. Whatever they are, realize that when you add more to your plate without taking others away, that plate will eventually be too crowded. Give yourself permission to say no without feeling guilty.

Birth's Effect on Time

I've often wondered if our daughters' births are connected to the way they experience time.

THE SPRING OF 1990, we anxiously awaited Allison's arrival. She was due on April 23 and wasn't born until May 1. Just as her long labor could not be rushed, as she grew, this "not rushing" theme followed her. She did things in her way and at her pace. Things got done, but in a calm manner without hurrying or being overly concerned about time.

Two years later, Cassie entered the world on June 18 with great ease, arriving precisely on her due date. Somehow, her punctual birth seemed to predict her feelings about time. Cass is always the first one ready to leave the house, encouraging the rest of us to "hurry up," or reminding us that we have "ten minutes" until it is time to leave. She is always on time, hates to be late, and gets ready quickly.

I'm sure there are other influences on the girls' sense of time that go beyond my observations. It fascinates me how their birth experiences seem to mirror their personalities and relationship to time. We all have traits we are born with. Respecting how to work with them enables us to fully appreciate our natural qualities.

Single vs. Multitasking
Reduce stress and increase focus by singletasking rather than multitasking.

WE ARE ASKED TO DO, process and fit more into every minute of our lives than ever before. With the amount of information and communication channels we have access to, including the Internet, TV, texting, instant messaging, newspapers, faxes, snail mail, voice mail, e-mail, landlines and cell phones, the barrage of input seems constant. How often do you find yourself talking on the phone while making dinner, emptying the dishwasher and answering questions from your family? Have you found yourself driving, texting and putting on make-up simultaneously? When was the last time you focused on one thing at a time?

I remember at some point we used to take pride in how many things we could do at once. Women in particular seem more adept at doing so. There is a price, though. That price is stress, which prolonged, can be a risk to our health. We also deny ourselves the joy of giving our complete attention to one idea, person or moment. This multi-doing creates a frenetic feeling within us. Our attention gets divided while our brains are taxed. We weren't designed to multitask, as suggested by some current research.

David Meyer, PhD, director of Brain, Cognition and Action Laboratory at the University of Michigan has extensively researched the effects of multitasking. He has concluded that not only is multitasking inefficient, but it also increases stress, can lead to dangerous health issues and can negatively effect short-term memory.[1] The next time you are tempted to do two things are once, consider giving yourself the gift of one.

Planned and Unplanned Time
Find your perfect balance between scheduled and float time.

EACH OF US PERCEIVES time differently. Some reject any kind of structure and like days to flow without committing to or planning anything more than a few hours ahead. Others prefer to have every moment scheduled and planned from morning to night. Those are the extremes and most of us fall somewhere in between.

I like a certain amount of planned time combined with unplanned time to catch my breath or take advantage of spur-of-the-moment opportunities. If too much of my life is scheduled, I feel as if I have no control over my time. I need to know that there are some days I don't have to wake up to

---

1   Bottom Line newsletter, May 1, 2009. "Multitasking and Stress" by Chris Woolston.
    Available online at http://www.yourhealthconnection.com/topic/multitasking/.

an alarm or be somewhere at a certain hour. I like to know that I am not so overscheduled that I sacrifice the opportunity of being spontaneous.

During vacations, I love that feeling of waking up when my body is rested and letting the day unfold without much of a plan. It's in such direct contrast to the rest of the year. I need and enjoy that change. Yet, I don't think I could live every day like that. I just want to have some days that way.

Identify what your preferences are and then design your time and schedule around them.

Focused Time

Using a timer can be extremely effective, especially if you are perpetually late, time challenged or need help focusing.

TO DEAL WITH THE MULTIPLE distractions in our environment, there is one tool I've found very helpful. My trusty buzzer helps me daily. Most mornings, I wake up, get showered and dressed, eat breakfast and have a short time remaining before I venture off to see clients. That morning time is usually spent returning calls, writing, responding to e-mails or working on a variety of other projects. While I enjoy the quiet time to focus on what I'm doing, I can become completely immersed and lose track of time. This is not good when I have appointments scheduled.

My favorite trick is to use a buzzer as my warning signal. I set it for ten minutes before I need to stop working. This gives me time to wrap up my thoughts, collect my stuff and get out the door on time. What I particularly love about using the timer is that it enables me to give my complete attention to what I'm doing without worrying about the clock. It enables me to focus and yet still leave the house on time.

Productivity
There are many ways to make downtime fun and productive.

IT IS POSSIBLE TO GET CREATIVE with your time. Here are some tips my clients have found helpful.

Do you find yourself keeping articles and newsletters that you'd like to read someday? Use your waiting time to catch up on some of your reading by creating a "Reading" folder and carrying it with you.

Do you have trouble sorting your mail on a regular basis? Bring a pile of unopened mail and use your waiting time to sort. Be ruthless and keep only the essential papers to file or act on. Recycle the rest.

Spring is a wonderful time for having picnics. Bring a tote bag of unread magazines. Eat, relax, and enjoy your surroundings while reading the latest articles.

Catch up on correspondence. It's fun to compose a handwritten letter and even nicer to receive one. Plant yourself in your favorite outdoor spot. Enjoy the spring air while writing to a special friend or relative.

We each have the same 24 hours.
What makes the difference
is how we use them.

Time Interrupters
Release yourself from excessive busyness.

SO MANY OF US FEEL as if we have more to accomplish in a day than time allows. We each have the same 24 hours. What makes the difference is how we use them. There are several things to be aware of that might help you be more effective with your days.

The telephone can be a major time-zapper. Just because the phone rings doesn't mean you have to answer it. If you're in the middle of something, let your answering machine or voicemail take a message. Return calls when you can give the caller your complete focus. On the day Allison was born, her pediatrician gave me a piece of advice I've never forgotten. He asked me if we owned an answering machine. We did. He said to me, "Use it! Right now, your baby is the most important thing in the world. She needs your full attention." While this was wonderful parenting advice, it extends beyond just raising kids. It's the idea about giving yourself permission to be clear about your priorities and the time to focus on them without interruptions.

E-mail can be another inefficiency. Check your messages several times a day rather than constantly. For most people this should be sufficient. If your e-mail program "dings" every time a new message comes in, consider turning off the sound so that you aren't tempted to check it.

Do you like to do everything yourself? Consider assigning tasks to people who can help you. Learning to delegate is a key to becoming a better manager of your time. I have discovered that by delegating to others, it increases my available free time and gives others the opportunity to contribute.

Remember the power of the two-letter word, "No!" Make sure you use it. Be wary of saying yes too often, especially if it negatively affects other areas of your life. Carefully choose the activities, projects and events you include in your schedule. This will enable you to complete what you've committed to, and feel less overwhelmed and more balanced.

Time to Appreciate
Allow yourself time to acknowledge your successes.

"STOP AND SMELL THE IRISES!" Some of you may be thinking, "Don't you mean *roses?*" Literally, for me, it is our irises that bloom each spring and grace our front path. Their sweet, candy-like scent is intoxicating. Since their blossoms are fleeting, I pause to smell them before continuing.

The concept of taking time for appreciating is an integral part of the organizing journey. Identify *your* irises. Congratulate yourself for making the call for organizing help or for keeping your junk drawer organized. Do a dance as you fill up another bag of papers to recycle. Don't miss an opportunity to appreciate the successes you've had and take the time to enjoy them, even if it's only for a moment.

III

Summer

"A perfect summer day is when the sun is shining,
the breeze is blowing, birds are singing and the lawn mower is broken."
— JAMES DENT

THE SKY IS BLUE AND A DULL LOW HUM OF A PLANE IS ABOVE.
THE THUMP OF A HAMMER IS AUDIBLE IN A NEARBY YARD. THERE
IS AN EVER-SO-SLIGHT BREEZE AND OCCASIONAL WHOOSHING
SOUND OF AN AIR CONDITIONER. THE AIR SMELLS GOOD. IT'S
NOT SWEET, BUT JUST CLEAN AND FRESH. IT'S NOT TOO HOT,
BUT WARM ENOUGH SO THAT NO GOOSEBUMPS APPEAR ON MY
BODY AS THE BREEZE BLOWS. I AM FEELING INCREDIBLY CALM
AND GRATEFUL THAT SUMMER HAS ARRIVED.

SEVEN

Getting Motivated

NORTON GOES

The motivation piece IS ESSENTIAL FOR MOVING US FOR-
WARD ON OUR ORGANIZING JOURNEY.

WHY DO WE DO ANYTHING IN LIFE? If we don't have
a reason or motivation, we will not take action. By knowing
why we are doing what we're doing and what benefits we hope
to derive, we can motivate ourselves to move ahead. If the
motivation is strong enough, it can help bring us through the
process. We can be motivated by positive or negative thoughts.
Figuring out your motivating factors will be key in helping you
attain your goals.

Have To vs. Want To
Being organized enables us to have more time for our "wants."

GETTING ORGANIZED WILL enable you to "spend less time doing the things you *have* to do and more time doing what you *want* to do," says *Real Simple* magazine. This statement echoes my organizing philosophy.

The organizing process can easily become an obsession. It's possible to lose sight of the truly important. Knowing your reasons for getting organized and the benefits you expect to derive are crucial. Maintaining focus on your goals will help keep you motivated through the organizing process.

I love to organize. In addition, many other things fill my life. I love being with my family and friends, writing, reading, dancing, singing, creating art, watching movies, and taking walks. Being organized *enough* gives me time to enjoy other parts of my life.

Organizing Ripple Effect
Sharing your organizing successes can inspire others.

AS A PROFESSIONAL ORGANIZER, I've encountered an interesting phenomenon. I call it the Organizing Ripple Effect. What happens when a pebble is thrown into a river? That single act creates many ripples in the water that extend far beyond the point of entry. Its influence is greater than the single "plunk."

A few summers back, a client shared her experience about a recent visit from a friend. During the visit, my client showed her friend the organizing work we had accomplished together. When the friend left and returned home, she felt inspired to also get organized. She used the rest of that summer to organize her home.

Other clients have shared similar stories. They've told me that merely mentioning to friends or family that they were working with a professional organizer influenced others to begin their own organizing and decluttering process. It is encouraging to realize that when others watch us accomplish our goals, they can be inspired to pursue theirs.

Visualizing to Motivate

Visualizing how you want your surroundings to be can help motivate you to take action.

SOMETIMES WE BECOME so overwhelmed by our surroundings that we become paralyzed. If you are unsure of how and where to begin, try a visualization technique.

Prepare by sitting down quietly with a paper and pen. Think about the details of your day from the moment you wake through bedtime. As you go through every step, jot down any rough spots you encounter. You might identify that your bathroom cabinet is so crowded it's difficult to open. Perhaps you have trouble finding the house keys to lock the door upon leaving. Whenever you find a "snag" in your day, no matter how large or small, visualize it and write it down.

Once you have collected a detailed list, select one small challenge to fix. It doesn't matter what you choose to do first. The key is that you identify an organizing project and implement a solution for that issue. Once it is solved, systematically find solutions one by one for the other challenges.

As you make these positive changes, notice how your stress level decreases. Solving the small issues will motivate you to approach some of your larger challenges.

Be kind to yourself. If you can't decide between organizing or going for a walk, take the walk, clear your head and then come back and reset your timer for a 15-minute organizing session.

Motivation Techniques
Find new ways to get motivated.

GETTING ORGANIZED is easier for some than for others. What happens when organizing is one of your challenges? When you want to get organized and don't feel like doing the work, how can you resolve the conflict? Here are a few techniques that might work for you.

Use a timer. Strive to organize for short yet regular 15- or 30-minute sessions. Organizing does not need to be done in marathon time blocks. Sometimes it is more bearable to do a difficult task if you are doing it in shorter increments. It becomes less of a big deal in your mind.

Celebrate your success. After accomplishing five short organizing sessions during a week, give yourself an appropriate reward. See a movie, have an ice cream cone or meet a friend for coffee. Rewarding yourself for commitment and progress can be a great motivating factor.

Be kind to yourself. If you can't decide between organizing or going for a walk, take the walk, clear your head and then come back and reset your timer for a 15-minute organizing session. The idea is to be consistent, work around the difficulties and forge ahead.

Building in the fun-factor can be motivating, too. Sometimes we work better when we have people with us to cheer us on and provide focus, so turn organizing into a social event. Ask a friend or professional to help with the process.

Motivation for Relaxation

One of the benefits of getting organized is having more time to relax.

CREATE A LEVEL OF ORGANIZATION that works so that you will have more time available to enjoy your life. Relaxing and rejuvenating is an important part of creating balance. Consider using some of these ideas as motivating forces along your organizing journey.

Nothing says "relax" more to me than resting peacefully in our hammock. I have spent many summer days resting, reading, writing, thinking or snuggling with my family in our hammock, which hangs between two tall oak trees. If you don't have a hammock, pick another comfortable spot like a couch, bed or chair. Stretch out and rest.

Sometimes the act of drinking tea can soothe the soul. Whether you choose iced or hot, pour a cup or glass of tea. Enjoy its temperature and aroma as you sit and sip it slowly, and allow yourself to decompress.

Watching a movie is another great way to relax. You can rent one and curl up in your pajamas or go out to a movie theater. Select a flick that will lift your spirits and make you smile.

The restorative powers of water always work for me. Being near or in water, whether it's an ocean, river, lake, waterfall, pool, bathtub or shower can have an incredibly calming effect. There is nothing quite like being at the ocean, watching the movement of the waves, or immersing myself in a pool or river. Find some water and unwind.

Finally, fresh air works wonders. Get outside. Take a walk. Ride a bike. Sit on a bench. Apply your sunscreen and let the summer air work its slowdown magic.

Create a level of organization that works so that you will have more time available to enjoy your life.

EIGHT

Enlisting Help

NORTON RETRIEVES

Finding the right type OF SUPPORT MIGHT BE THE PUZZLE PIECE YOU'VE BEEN SEARCHING FOR.

HAVE YOU BEEN FRUSTRATED by unsuccessful attempts to get organized? Knowing when to enlist help is often the key component of success. For many, organizing works more effectively when it is done as a social activity. The right person can provide encouragement, nudge you past the overwhelmed stage, monitor your progress, establish accountability and help you stay focused. An organizing buddy may be exactly what you need for getting the results you desire.

Organizing Buddies
*The organizing process can be less overwhelming with the help of
an organizing buddy.*

CLIENTS OFTEN SAY, "I couldn't have done this without
you!" or "I accomplish so much more when you are working
with me." Very often, what clients are experiencing is *body dou-
bling.* This phenomenon is described in Judith Kolberg's book,
*What Every Professional Organizer Needs to Know About Chronic
Disorganization.*

Quietly standing next to clients, I watched them process desk papers that prior to my arrival were overwhelming
them. I witnessed them change from paralyzed to mobilized.
My physical presence functions as a body double, a "human
anchor," as organizing coach Linda Anderson described. My
clients moved past feeling overwhelmed and became energized
to take action.

One client explained it wasn't that she didn't know how
to organize, but she just needed someone to be with her. She
needed an "organizing buddy." As a professional organizer, I
try to be as chameleon-like as possible, mirroring my clients'
energy while simultaneously helping them stay focused and
move forward toward their goals.

One client explained it wasn't that she didn't know how to organize, but she just needed someone to be with her. She needed an "organizing buddy."

In This Together
You are not alone. Many people are organizationally challenged.

MANY TIMES CLIENTS have asked me questions like, "What is wrong with me?" "Why can't I get organized without someone else's help?" or, "Why is everyone else organized except me?" They wonder if they are beyond help. Some have shared feelings of disappointment, doubt, low self-esteem, and loneliness. Especially for the organizationally challenged, these thoughts can be common. There are many people who struggle with organizing issues.

Perhaps you are challenged or know someone who is. Be reassured that you are not alone. We each have different gifts and strengths. There is no shame in asking for help in areas that you find difficult.

Professional Organizer's Role
Organizing help is not a one-size-fits-all role.

ONE RECENT SUMMER DAY, a discussion with one of my clients caused me to rethink some of my assumptions. My client was disturbed by my premise, which was that if you made organizing your priority, you would learn the necessary skills. She shared that while organizing is a priority for her, she felt that she would *never* be able to acquire those skills.

When I began organizing, I believed that while not everyone was organized, organizing was a teachable skill. However, as time has passed and I've had the opportunity to work with hundreds of clients. I realize that while I do teach organizing skills to some, I also function in other roles.

For some clients, I am a support person. Organizing is difficult for them because of physical, emotional, or medical challenges. I become the organizing ingredient in their lives. Other clients are organized, yet are time-poor. Again, I support them in a different manner where they delegate organizing projects to me. Some clients immerse themselves in the organizing process. They acquire organizing skills by working side-by-side with me. Lastly, some use my services to help them maintain and tweak established systems.

My objective is always the same: to make a positive difference and help others with their unique organizing challenges. Whatever my role, I am grateful to be a part of their lives.

Enlisting Help or Not

We view organizing in different ways. Not everyone wants or needs help getting organized.

THE ORGANIZING INDUSTRY bristled at the 2007 *New York Times* article, "Saying Yes to Mess." The article negatively portrayed our profession, and I felt compelled to write about this. As an industry, we must be sensitive to the fact that not everyone desires to get organized. In fact, many people thrive in a cluttered environment. As a professional organizer, however, I am interested in working with people who seek change. I understand that not everyone wants or needs my help.

What the article missed was that most organizers are compassionate, creative, empathetic people who love to help others. We know that people are different and have varying needs, and that there is no single, "right" method of organizing. I focus on partnering with clients who want my expertise, insights, and help finding creative solutions to their specific organizing challenges.

Chronic Disorganization

If getting and staying organized has been a consistent lifelong struggle, you might be chronically disorganized.

CHRONIC DISORGANIZATION is a term developed by Judith Kolberg, founder of the National Study Group on Chronic Disorganization. There are four hallmarks of chronic disorganization: a history of being disorganized, self-help efforts to change that have been unsuccessful, disorganization that negatively affects the quality of your daily life, and a future expectation of disorganization.

If you identify with any of these descriptions, you may be chronically disorganized. If so, traditional methods of linear organizing may not work for you. Enlisting outside support such as therapists, family, friends or professional organizers educated in working with chronically disorganized people could have a positive effect on your organizing success.

Hiring a Professional Organizer
Ask lots of questions before hiring a professional organizer.

CLARIFYING YOUR NEEDS will help you find a professional organizer who is right for you. What kind of organizing help do you need? There is a wide range of organizing specialties. Some organizers specialize in residential or business organizing. Some organize papers while others orchestrate moves. Some organizers are generalists while others specialize in working with chronically disorganized clients.

Think about your organizing challenges. Do you need assistance with a single, short-term project such as organizing a closet or filing system? Instead, do you need ongoing support with a more complex, long-term project such as organizing an entire household?

Do you have the time and financial resources to invest in your organizing goals? Realize that you will be dedicating time to accomplish your goals. If you hire a professional to help, you will be making an investment in your future and allocating funds to do so.

Has organizing always been a challenge for you? If you have a history of disorganization and challenges with getting organized, you might achieve better results by enlisting the help of a professional organizer. Consider finding an organizer who specializes in working with chronically disorganized clients. Above all, ask good questions and consider the following aspects of working with a professional.

The initial conversations you have with an organizer can be an indicator how well your relationship will work down the road. Did you find the organizer through a referral, ad,

*If you have a history of
disorganization and challenges with
getting organized, you might achieve
better results by enlisting the help of
a professional organizer.*

professional association, article or Internet search? When you first communicated with the organizer, did he or she answer all your questions? Did the organizer understand your unique challenges and organizing goals? Was the organizer nonjudgmental? Would you enjoy working together?

The availability factor is important. Even though organizing is part of a service industry geared towards clients, individual businesses are structured differently. Are your schedules compatible? Can the organizer accommodate your needs? Do you want to work with the organizer evenings or weekends? If so, is the organizer available then?

Research will enable you to make a more informed decision. Did you interview more than one organizer? Organizers have different personalities, business practices and methodologies. It might be beneficial to contact several organizers to compare those differences. Did you ask the organizer for references? If so, consider the type of work he or she did with those clients and the longevity of those relationships. What insights did the clients share? Does the organizer have a Website? If so, did you view it to learn more? What impressions did you have?

Do not ignore your intuition. Let it help guide you. What does your inner voice tell you about the organizer? Did you feel hopeful or discouraged after your conversation?

The level of the organizer's education and experience can also have an effect on your organizing success. What type of special education or training does the organizer have? How many years has the organizer been in business? What was their previous occupation? Do they continue to educate themselves on organizing issues and trends? Do they use resources such as other professionals, publications or products that they will share with you? Do they have membership in professional organizing associations? The more engaged the organizer is with their industry, the more value they can offer.

There are thousands of organizers throughout the world and each is as unique as the clients they serve. Like you, organizers want the relationship to be successful. If they are not suited to you, keep searching until you find an organizer who can better meet your needs. By considering some of these questions, you can find the organizer who is the right fit for you.[1]

Finding Help
Professional associations have a wealth of information and resources.

SEVERAL ORGANIZATIONS provide a range of information about organizing issues and have directories for locating professional organizers in your area.

Australasian Association of Professional Organisers Inc. (www.aapo.org.au)
AAPO is a comprised of professional organizers in Australia and New Zealand. They focus on educating the public about professional organizing and promoting services to their members. AAPO also helps professional organizers develop new skills and meet required standards of practice.

---

1 Linda Samuels wrote *How Do I Find A Professional Organizer Who Is Right For Me?* for NSGCD. That version is available through http://www.nsgcd.org under Fact Sheets.

National Association of Professional Organizers (www.napo.net)

NAPO is an international association based in the United States. Their Website includes organizing tips and resources for finding professional organizers. Education and certification are available for organizers through teleclasses and conferences.

National Study Group on Chronic Disorganization (www.nsgcd.org)

NSGCD is an international association based in the United States. Their Website has information geared for the chronically disorganized population and the professionals who work with them. The site includes FAQs, fact sheets, publications, Speakers Bureau information and other resources such as how to find professional organizers and related professionals. Education and certification are available for professional organizers and related professionals through teleclasses, publications and conferences.

Professional Organizers of Canada (www.organizersincanada.com)

POC is an international association based in Canada. Their Website has FAQs and resources for finding Canadian-based professional organizers. Education is available for professional organizers through teleclasses and conferences.

NINE

Discovering Success Secrets

NORTON SHOPS

Organizing success RANGES FROM FINDING THAT PERFECT CONTAINER TO DEVELOPING AN "I CAN" ATTITUDE.

THERE ARE CORE ORGANIZING success secrets. You may already be incorporating some of them into your life. As you begin to combine all the concepts, your potential for achieving your organizing goals increases dramatically.

Organizing Success Secrets

To maximize your organizing success, integrate these core concepts into your life.

DEVELOP A POSITIVE ATTITUDE. When you send your brain the "I can" message, possibilities unfold and enable you to accomplish so much more. Maintaining a good attitude is the first step in moving past your frustration and towards your organizing goals.

Visualize the results of your organizing efforts. Keep an image in mind of what your environment will look or feel like when you have better control over your life. Having a physical or mental picture of your goal will help motivate you to reach it.

Begin and things become possible. You can't just *think* about getting organized. You must also take action. Don't permit excuses. Remember that the fear of doing is often more intimidating than the actual work. Taking action will energize you; action promotes success, which encourages more action.

Don't forget to enlist the help of an organizing buddy. If you can't face your organizing challenges on your own, find someone to help you through the process. Once again, this can be a professional or a friend. Your buddy will provide encouragement and focus, and help you move past the overwhelmed phase.

Use lists to keep on track. They will help you maintain focus, unclutter your mind and organize your thoughts for action. Refer to your lists several times throughout the day, including first thing in the morning and before going to bed.

Learn to master the minutes. Use small blocks of time. We often don't have large amounts of uninterrupted time to take care of things, so ask yourself, "What can be

Develop a positive attitude.
When you send your brain the
"I can" message, possibilities
unfold and enable you to
accomplish so much more.

accomplished in ten minutes?" You can organize a drawer, clear out your wallet, write a note to a friend or read a story to your child. In five minutes, you can make a few phone calls, sort your mail or empty the dishwasher. In one minute you can review your to-do list, make your bed or stop and enjoy the warm summer air.

Is clutter getting in your way? Lessen the stuff and you will find it easier to stay organized. Make room for things you truly want. Discard unwanted and unused belongings. Ask yourself questions like, "Do I need to be the keeper of this paper?" "If I tossed it, could I get it again?" "Do I really need to keep the clothes that haven't fit me for over five years?" "Is this item useful or is it just taking up space?" "Could someone else benefit from having it?" After decluttering, it is common to experience feelings of relief, happiness and hope.

Preparation is critical. Take time to think through what you want to accomplish. Don't wait until the last minute to do things. For example, before going to sleep, review what needs to be done the following day. Ask yourself if there is anything that you can do now to help make tomorrow run more smoothly.

Learning to delegate is another success secret. Enlist the help of others, including your children. What can be delegated to give you more free time and reduce your stress? Doing everything yourself can cause exhaustion, resentfulness and inefficiency. Instead, you can hire or barter with others to do cleaning, cooking, laundry, errands, childcare, carpooling, yard work, filing, bill-paying or organizing.

Rejuvenation is essential. Make time to take care of yourself. Understand what makes you feel good and then reserve the time to do it. This is not selfish; it's necessary. It can be simple or more elaborate, but it is necessary to your well-being. Exercise, take a walk, read a book or take a few moments to reflect about the joys and challenges of the day. Reconnect with yourself. This will replenish your energy and enable you to move ahead feeling refreshed.

The Magic Wand Revisited

The maintenance ingredient is an essential element in the organizing process.

YEARS AGO, A CLIENT ASKED me if I had a magic wand. She wanted me to wave it and instantly organize everything. One recent summer, another client asked me a similar question, but with a twist. She too asked, "Do you have a magic wand to organize everything with the flick of your wrist?" She added, "Can you make my clutter go away and *never* come back?"

In that question, she identified an essential principle of organizing. Even if you organize, you'll have to maintain what you've done. Organizing is similar to doing laundry or going grocery shopping. Doing it once isn't enough. It requires a consistent, ongoing effort that requires not just creating, but also *maintaining* organizing systems.

Similar to magic, organizing involves transformation. It is during the organizing process that amazing results are accomplished. While I don't possess a magic wand, it is wonderful when clients experience a magical feeling.

The Organizing Gene

Some of you were probably "born organized," while others feel as if organizing has been a lifelong challenge.

HAVE YOU EVER WONDERED whether there is an organizing gene? With our daughters, we noticed differences in their organizing abilities from early on. When Allison was born, I started thinking about the existence of an organizing gene. As we marveled at her development, we were amazed at how organized she appeared. Two years later, when Cassie was born, we noticed similar traits.

Interestingly enough, it wasn't until Allison began kindergarten that we noticed she was struggling with staying organized. She had difficulty keeping track of her belongings. Without meaning to, I had been compensating for her. Once I recognized this, rather than continuing to organize for her, I began to share some organizing skills. For the next few years, I worked on teaching her how to group her belongings, set up systems, and follow through with tasks.

Cassie seemed to be born organized. She naturally developed her own methods for remembering and grouping things without much help from me, and gravitated towards a certain amount of order. At an early age, if she opened a drawer, she'd automatically close it when finished. If I called to her when she was in the middle of a task, she'd respond with, "Just a minute, Mom!" and finish what she was doing before moving on. She rarely lost or misplaced things.

Many clients have placed getting organized as a high priority. I feel privileged to participate in their journey. Being organized is valuable skill that enables us to function in a complex world. For years, I took my organizing abilities for granted, giving no more thought to them than I do to my brown eyes or curly hair. At a point, I recognized how my organizing skills had helped me in many parts of my life. We each have special gifts. Yours might be that you are artistic, great with people, or a big-picture thinker. It is essential to identify, appreciate and share your gifts.

How is this relevant to you? My basic belief about organizing is that some of us were born with this strength and some were not. Is there an organizing gene? I don't know the scientific answer. Whether or not a gene exists is not what matters. Organizing is a teachable skill for most who want to learn it (notice that I say "most"). You can cultivate the tools needed to develop those skills. If you are organizationally challenged, you can enlist help from others who do have the skills.

Variations on Organizing Success

Our goals vary as widely as our definition of organizing success.

WHAT DOES ORGANIZING success look like? As you can imagine, it is different for each person. Since we begin with assorted challenges and goals, our personal definition of success varies greatly.

For some, organizing success is a clear desk without any piles of paper on it. Some are satisfied knowing where to find their keys. To others, success is a clothing closet in which everything can be easily accessed and all the extraneous items are gone. Others view success as feeling in charge of their time and schedule. No more missed appointments; no more overscheduling without time to breathe. Some see success as having a filing system for papers and paying bills on time. Some define success as a house where every room, drawer, closet, nook and cranny is clutter-free. They want all their possessions to have a place to go. They want the tension between kids, spouses, friends and other family members to disappear as they get their homes and lives organized. Success means not feeling overwhelmed by their stuff, their time and their lives.

Create your version of organizing success and commit the time and resources to achieve it.

When you find yourself overwhelmed by errands, organizing projects and appointments, pause long enough to connect with the ones you love.

Gratitude

When you are feeling overwhelmed, don't underestimate your human connections.

GRATITUDE IS AN IMPORTANT part of life. I often think about how thankful I am for the special people in my life.

You might be wondering, "How does this relate to organizing?" When we make time to create our homes and spaces the way we envision, when we plan our days to encompass "our" people and meaningful events, we integrate self-care. When we care for ourselves, we are better able to have compassion and energy for others. While I admit that as an organizer, finding the perfect storage container excites me, one of the *essential* organizing ingredients is making the time to celebrate and love ourselves along with the people that mean so much to us. When you find yourself overwhelmed by errands, organizing projects and appointments, pause long enough to connect with the ones you love. Be grateful for the wonderful people in your life.

IV

Fall

"The best time to plant a tree is twenty years ago.
The second best time is now."
—AFRICAN PROVERB

WHEN I NOTICE THE FIRST FEW LEAVES BEGINNING TO TURN COLOR, IT'S NATURE'S SIGNAL THAT CHANGE IS UPON US. I FIND IT FASCINATING THAT COMPLETE TRANSFORMATION DOESN'T HAPPEN OVERNIGHT. THE PROCESS IS SLOW UNTIL ONE DAY YOU REALIZE THAT THE GREEN OF SUMMER HAS TURNED TO ORANGES, YELLOWS AND REDS OF FALL. THIS GRADUAL SHIFT HELPS US ADJUST NOT ONLY TO THE NEW SEASON, BUT ALSO TO THE CHANGES THAT ARE HAPPENING IN OUR OWN LIVES.

TEN

Possibility Thinking

NORTON VACATIONS

It is our dream OF WHAT IS POSSIBLE THAT GIVES US HOPE.

WHEN WE ENVISION positive outcomes, relationships and lives, we are using possibility thinking. When we let ourselves imagine what is possible, even if we've had a history of disappointments, we allow positive energy to enter our thoughts and actions. Dreaming is just as essential as taking action.

Possibility Thinking

Uncertain times have inspired me to be more creative, embrace new ideas and work even harder at balancing life.

MAYBE IT'S THE SHIFT to the fall season. Maybe it's that uncertainty has jostled me from being complacent. Whatever it is, I'm feeling hopeful. While nothing is certain (and by the way it never was), this feels like a time of opportunity. This is a time to go beyond where we're comfortable. Establish time to explore ideas that have been collecting on lists for too long. Make time to regroup and refocus. Find time to declutter the mind, the home or the office to make room for the "what ifs." As the gorgeous fall leaves display their brilliance, let the magic of this season fill you with hope, creativity and possibility thinking.

Find time to declutter the mind, the home or the office to make room for the "what ifs."

Dream Away
*Be the director of your story and think about what you want to
incorporate in your life.*

ORGANIZING ISN'T JUST about sorting papers, editing closets, and rearranging the junk drawer. It's also about having the
level of order that's comfortable for you. Getting organized will
reduce the stress of life's details, enable you to accomplish some
larger goals and give you more time to embrace your passions.
It's essential to let dreaming be part of the organizing process.
There are several ways to start the dream juices flowing.

Dream small. If you had an extra 30 minutes free each day,
how would you use that time? Would you read a book, take a
walk or have coffee with a friend? If 30 extra minutes a day
seems like a tremendous gift, begin here. Once you've managed to secure your extra 30 minutes, think about moving on
to bigger goals.

Dream moderately. If there are 52 weekends per year and
you reserved just four of them to complete a short-term project, what would it be? Sometimes we think about "projects"
we'd like to do and never schedule the time to get them done.
With a little advance-planning and commitment, it is possible
to accomplish some of these dreams.

Dream big. If time, money or circumstance weren't challenges, what would you want to accomplish? Let your mind
dream without criticism or judgment. Often we tend to discourage ourselves before even taking our first steps forward.
Try to suspend all negativity; there is no harm in dreaming and
wishing. Identifying what you'd like comes before any action
can occur.

Think Again
Our attitude can make or break the outcome.

HENRY FORD SAID, "Whether you think you can or think you can't—you are right." How often does your inner voice whisper negative messages? Does that voice say you are going to fail even before you've begun? Does it tell you that you've been unsuccessful before, and you shouldn't think you'll succeed this time? In contrast, perhaps your inner voice is cheering you on. Is it telling you that you will succeed no matter what? Is the voice saying that your past failures are not an indicator of your future successes?

With many people, I often hear them repeating more negative messages than positive ones. Each time we repeat a negative message, it becomes more ingrained in our beliefs, and we sabotage ourselves. Challenge yourself to stop the negativity and to instead concentrate on positive thoughts. Even if you don't believe that you are capable of adopting new habits and behaviors, try anyway. If you speak and think positive thoughts, soon you will begin believing them. Every time you hear that negative voice, identify it, stop it from speaking and turn the message into something positive.

There is joy to be found at every stage in the organizing process. Be open to the possibilities.

Joyful Possibilities
Discover the joy in the organizing process— be it the impetus, the struggle or the result.

I WORK WITH CLIENTS who want to get organized and have reached out for help. They find joy in various stages of the organizing process. Some are energized by just the thought of getting organized. At first contact, they are already hopeful about how we can work together to accomplish their organizational goals. They expect a positive outcome.

Others feel overwhelmed at first. In addition, they might feel hopeless and skeptical about anyone's ability to help them. They might begin the organizing process with negative feelings. Once we begin taking action, however, their attitudes slowly shift. The forward motion erases the feeling of being overwhelmed and enables their joy to surface.

Some only feel satisfied after they've accomplished their goals. They have more difficultly acknowledging their successes along the way. Their negativity persists for longer. When they are able to step back and recognize their accomplishments, they allow themselves to be happy.

There is joy to be found at every stage in the organizing process. Be open to the possibilities.

It's essential to let dreaming be part of the organizing process.

ELEVEN

Wonderfully Human

NORTON FOCUSES

Our humanity is apparent IN WHO WE LOVE, THE MIS-
TAKES WE MAKE AND THE WAYS WE FORGIVE.

WE ARE NOT MACHINES or computers. We are human beings
that make mistakes. We have the ability to pursue goals, fail
and try again anyway. We have the capacity to forgive others
and ourselves, find humor at the darkest moments and focus
on what is important. These qualities connect us and make us
wonderfully human.

The List

It's not just about the list.

OUR TO-DO LISTS can seem daunting. In addition, lists have a way of growing. Just when one list is near completion and you are actually beginning to feel that you've accomplished a great deal, new items pop onto the list, begging for your time and attention.

One fall I came to a realization that my list was extremely ambitious. My goal was to use the fall to tackle it. Halfway through the season, I noticed that only one item had been checked off and the clock was ticking. It made me feel anxious and pressured. I berated myself for not doing enough.

My list eventually gets done, but not always in the timeframe I set. Finding balance between doing and being is important.

At that point, I remembered that the list was only part of the equation. It was also important to enjoy the beautiful fall season. My list would eventually get done, but not necessarily in the timeframe I'd set. Finding balance between *doing* and *being* was important. By fall's end, I *did* manage to accomplish about half of my list.

In accepting balance, I adjusted the self-imposed deadline, paced myself and partook in life's serendipities.

Our Stuff

It is not the "dressing" of life, but the core of who we are that matters most.

PEOPLE WHO HAVE NOT visited my family often wonder what our house is like. Some imagine that we live a life without clutter or objects. On the contrary, our home is filled with an assortment of colors and things, with a predominance of purple. We have many collections including Pez dispensers, books, artwork, miniatures, photographs, porcelain signs, trains and more. Our home is filled with physical possessions that we enjoy.

That said, I understand that life is not about the things I own. While our objects are fun to look at and use, they do not overwhelm my life. I've found a comfortable balance between owning physical items and the living of my life. It is who I am, the experiences I have, and the people I love who take priority over the "stuff."

Organize for Comfort, Not Obsession
Be careful that your desire to get organized doesn't take the joy out of life.

IN A 2001 BOTTOM LINE article by Joe Kita, I read a compelling passage. The article was about life lessons parents can share with their children. Kita's advice was to "be spontaneous." He said that while being organized is fine, it can cause stress and excess pressure if you place too much emphasis on it. It can take some of the joy out of life.

You may think that these are odd thoughts for an organizer to share. After all, being organized and helping others to do the same is one of my passions. However, I interpret Kita's words to mean "keep perspective and balance." Organize your life and surroundings enough to help your days flow more easily. Equally important is to be open to the unexpected change of plans, to be flexible and spontaneous.

In other words, pause to smell the crisp air, open your eyes to behold the incredible fall colors, play a game with your kids, hug your loved ones often and tell them how much you love them, interrupt your routine to make room for the "what ifs."

Flexibility and spontaneity are not my strengths; I work at embracing them. I encourage each of you, as you pursue your organizing balance, to make sure you leave some time unplanned, too. Organize for comfort, but not obsession. Embrace the joy that surrounds you. Wonderful things will transpire.

Life with Computers

Pay attention to the effects of your time spent with computers.

MANY OF YOU will relate to this. I spend a fair amount of time using my computer for e-mailing, Internet surfing, book-keeping, researching and writing. One fall Saturday, I spent most of that day away from my computer. Instead of sitting in front of the monitor, I used the time to create, wrap gifts and write with paper and pen instead of a keyboard. I loved my low-tech time.

At the end of the day, I returned to my computer to do some work. I could actually feel a shift in my brain. It felt as if a switch had flipped and my brain was processing differently. I don't know how else to describe this sensation, other than to say it was noticeable. It was almost a strain to be at the computer after doing the other creative, hands-on projects. I made a mental note that it's essential for me to strive for a better balance between computer and offline time. My head and heart seem to crave this in the same way I need food for nourishment.

Organizing and Stress
You can feel calmer by organizing.

SOMETIMES WHEN I FEEL STRESSED, I begin organizing, straightening and humming. It's not a conscious act, but something I've become aware of. I never thought much about it until I came across an article by nutritional consultant Jane Cole-Hamilton of Wellspring Seminars.[1] She said that if you understand which brain hemisphere is experiencing stress, you can do specific activities to relieve that stress. For example, if you feel emotionally overwhelmed, your stress is coming from the right hemisphere, which is the creative, emotional side. By organizing or doing math, for example, your brain switches over to the left side. Your right side will calm down, and you'll eliminate stress.

If you feel time-stressed and overburdened, the left hemisphere of the brain is involved. By singing or playing a sport, the right side of your brain will be activated, and this will have a calming, stress-reducing effect on the left side of your brain.

I wonder whether by singing and organizing simultaneously, you can eliminate all stress?

---

1 "Outsmarting Stress" by Jane Cole Hamilton, Wellspring Seminar. Knowledge Heaquarters online newsletter, September 2008 Vol 11-9; http://www.e-tutor.com/eNews/issue0908

Organizing and Humor
Finding humor in life and laughing can reduce stress and improve your sense of well-being.

IN OUR HOUSEHOLD, humor goes a long way in promoting harmony and diffusing some challenging moments. Nothing feels better than laughing so hard that tears roll down our faces. Sometimes we can take ourselves so seriously that we eliminate opportunities for laughter's positive effects. Instead, if we are open to it, humor can help us negotiate difficult moments and create strong bonds with one another.

Humor is also important in the organizing work I do. Often the clients who experience considerable stress over their organizing and life challenges find relief in appropriate moments of humor. Being able to laugh together over the simplest of things can help take the edge off of stress.

Organizing and Love
While organization helps with life's daily management, it also enables us to focus on what is most precious.

FALL ARRIVED MORE QUICKLY this year, bringing its changing leaves and cooler air. It also brought the passing of my mother-in-law, Sunny. My thoughts keep returning to her. During the last few years she simplified her life and made sure things were in order for her family. In our grief, I was so grateful that she took the time and care to do this for us.

Sunny derived great pleasure from having an organized home. She had an incredible talent for space planning and utilization. Knowing how much I shared her appreciation for organizing, she loved showing me her inventive solutions; for instance, she was a master at repurposing items. And further, her organization wasn't just about how she kept her home, but also about the ways she celebrated her family—she never missed birthdays, anniversaries and special occasions. Photos and albums of all her loved ones graced the interior of her home. While her organization helped in the daily management of life, it really enabled her to focus on what was most precious to her: time enjoying her family and friends.

Life dealt her many challenges. I admired her perseverance, devotion to family, sense of humor and directness. I am grateful that she was in my life and I will miss her.

Wonderfully Human

While our lives are punctuated by the "big" events, in fact, the daily moments define us.

THERE ARE MILESTONES in life that make us reflect. This past fall I found myself thinking back when Allison turned 16. When I asked her how she felt about this special event, she responded, "Mom, I'm just one day older than yesterday." For me, this particular birthday marked a significant juncture.

To honor this crossing, I created a journal for her. It included her photos, art, poetry, and writing. So typical for projects of this nature, the idea for its creation occupied my thoughts for months. However, as often happens, the time I left to actually create the album was much too short. Translated, that means I was up very late the night before her birthday rushing to complete the project. Yes, you guessed it: The organizer procrastinated.

When I gave her the journal the next morning, I noticed that I had made some typos. This upset me because I wanted the gift to be perfect.

We can always make improvements, but it's important to know when to just let things be.

Allison loved the journal. Despite the typos, she didn't focus on the mistakes. Instead, she enjoyed the gift as it was. She knew that the intent was not diminished by a few errors. I told her that I'd made some mistakes and wanted to fix them. She said, "It's *my* album! I won't let you." She understood that it was just as important for me as it was for her to recognize that we all make mistakes. Sometimes our personal best is good enough.

We can always make improvements, but it's important to know when to just let things be. Her reminder and gift to me was that we are all wonderfully human, not perfect. The typos remained as evidence of our humanity.

TWELVE

Life Balance

NORTON ENJOYS

Life balance IS LIKE A SEESAW. IT HAS ITS UPS, DOWNS AND
THE OCCASIONAL PERFECT MIDPOINT.

WHAT MAKES US feel balanced? Is it having the time to
incorporate our passions along with the responsibilities we've
accepted? Is it having harmony between relaxation and work?
Is it when all aspects of our lives seem to flow with one another?
When we achieve that sense of balance, it seems to exist for
just a period. A shift occurs and that balance disappears. We
then seek out ways to find a new balanced state.

Balance Is a Choice

We can't control everything, but we can make decisions about what is important and how we use our time.

MY MOM IS AN inspiration to me. She is passionate about life. She continues to ask important questions to make sure that her daily choices are in alignment with her priorities and values. Especially when she's preparing for the fall, we have conversations about life balance. I've listened as she figured out how many things she wanted to include in her schedule, why she wanted them, if they were meaningful and if they added or detracted from what was important to her. She's included me many times in her thinking process. Even at the ripe young age of 80, she continues to ask questions about how she spends her days.

This life skill of creating balance has been passed on to our family. While our daughters' lives are also full, they have breathing time and have deliberately chosen not to over-schedule. When Allison was 12, she found herself involved in too many extracurricular activities. On her own, she decided to make some changes. She explained to me that while she didn't like to "quit" things, she felt overwhelmed. She wanted to enjoy each activity, and have time for her schoolwork and friends without feeling rushed and stressed. She carefully examined her schedule and talked with us about possible adjustments she could make to create a better balance.

We've watched Cassie also decide out how to combine her passions, schoolwork and social life. In 11th grade, she worked diligently with her guidance counselor to design a schedule that combined challenging classes with school requirements,

Balance is a choice. Balance is not something to be achieved once and never reexamined. It's like a dance, constantly moving.

and also integrated classes she loved. Outside of school, she had many other activities. Certain time periods became over-scheduled, but Cassie thought carefully about her choices and opted to include certain things anyway. During the more stressful times, she reminded herself that it was just for a short period of time and that soon, one activity would end, giving her back some free time.

Balance is a choice. Balance is not something to be achieved once and never reexamined. It's like a dance, constantly moving. A full life requires us to be selective. Creating a balance that works for us enables us to enjoy the time we've been given.

Mindful Actions

Achieving a comfortable balance isn't easy. Awareness comes first, followed by different and deliberate choices.

THE CRISPNESS OF FALL arrived and summer vacation was just a memory. My time away continued to influence my thinking as I reflected back. During vacation, alarm clocks were turned off and instead I woke naturally. I let each day unfold gently without any big plans. After several days, I could actually feel myself slow down. As my movements and think-ing relaxed, it became all too obvious that my pace prior to vacation had been too intense. It was noticeable how much I enjoyed my less frenetic self.

Upon returning home and gearing up for fall activities, maintaining a slower speed was more difficult. I made a con-scious effort to be mindful of my actions and choices. I was determined to be more aware of how I moved through my day.

When I felt myself driving quickly, I slowed down. When I was tired at the end of the day, I let myself "just be" rather than push to complete one more item on my list.

I come from a long line of doers. At 80, my mom can still run rings around me. Our family joke is that she has so much energy, she sleeps with her eyes open. So my need to go, go, go is deeply ingrained. While there's nothing wrong with that, I've realized that pacing is essential. Some pressures are real while others are self-imposed. I try to question all of them, especially the self-imposed ones. If they are important, is quickness also required, or can I slow down and allow myself to feel more balanced?

After I returned from vacation, maintaining a slower pace was challenging. I continued my pursuit for a better balance anyway.

Balancing Act
The balance shifts at various points in our lives.

THERE ARE TIMES of near-perfect balance, times to adjust and times that we become ridiculously out of balance. It may be possible to do it all, but not simultaneously. Choices have to be made. With this premise, I accept where I am, yet pay attention to the time needed to transition into another phase.

When I began my organizing business in 1993, I had an infant and a toddler, commuted to New York City for a part-time job, developed my organizing business, hosted bimonthly Cajun dance parties at our home, took business classes at night and juggled a variety of other activities. My husband was self-employed and his work schedule was demanding. Was our life hectic and insane? Absolutely!

There came a point where I had no balance between family and work. I wanted to enjoy all aspects of my life (the girls, my husband, the parties, the new business venture) but instead I struggled with the tasks and responsibilities of each day. My increasing stress level forced me to examine my choices. I started to make changes and adjusted my balance closer to center.

To achieve my goal, I resigned from my job in the city in order to develop my organizing business. I established specific business hours so that work was distinctly separate from family time. We took a break from hosting the Cajun dance parties. Making those changes enabled me to improve my focus and reduce stress. When I was with my family, I was with them 100 percent. When I was with clients, I gave them my full attention. I've continued to strive for this goal of being in the moment.

After many years of refining, I've been able to integrate my business and family life. Some of the choices I've made include rarely working weekends, not accepting organizing projects with quick deadlines, and having a mix of long- and short-term clients. While I am passionate about my organizing business and clients, I know that my family absolutely comes first. Knowing this gives me clarity to make decisions.

Aside from the conceptual issues of balance, there are practical things I do to maintain harmony. My calendar (on my PDA) is color-coded. At a glance, I can visually see how my time is being scheduled. In addition, our family has a healthy mix of time together and apart. This includes weekly dates with my husband, some family time together each weekend, dinners together when possible and individual time spent with hobbies, friends and extended family.

Using "yes" and "no" in moderation has been another key ingredient in keeping a healthy life balance. I carefully choose volunteer activities so that I don't say yes to projects that will take too much time away from my current commitments. There are times, as admitted earlier, that I use the "y" word more than I'd like. I'm a work in progress.

During every 24-hour period, a third of our time is spent sleeping. This makes our waking hours even more precious. Balance is not something that can be achieved once and never reexamined. An abundant life requires us to be selective so that we can appreciate each day to its fullest.

The Balance of Organizing

Organize in moderation today so that you can play more tomorrow.

THERE IS NOTHING wrong with wanting to get organized. In fact, by achieving a certain amount of order in your life, you will be able to carve out more time for enjoyment. Organizing is just a means to an end. The idea is to create a schedule and environment that supports your life.

Organizing only becomes a problem when the act of doing it becomes an obsession that takes us away from the life we want to live. The objective is getting organized *enough* so that you can still have time for all the other things that are important to you. It's all about finding *your* right balance.

Rock River
Find a source to restore your balance and replenish your soul.

ORGANIZING EXTENDS beyond having a place for everything. It's also about finding balance, discovering places and people that renew your energy. One of my favorite places to visit in any season is Rock River. I go there to reconnect with family, nature, and myself. My favorite way to get to the river is by taking a 20-minute walk down my block and through the woods. It is particularly beautiful in the fall when I see above me the intense colors on the trees and I hear beneath my feet the crunchy leaves as I walk.

I've spent many hours at Rock River sitting, swimming, eating, thinking, writing, and just being in this most incredible place. Why is it so special? I climb out onto the rocks and plunk myself right down in the middle of the river. I dip my toes in the cool water or submerge myself completely on a hot day. After being there awhile, I release all thoughts and concerns and find myself just existing, sensing the water, the sun, and the air. I become part of the river as it flows past me downstream. I've also been there many times with my family. We've gone swimming, picnicked, talked, and laughed. It's impossible to spend time at Rock River without feeling rejuvenated.

As you work on your organizing goals, remember to include time to recharge.

Organizing extends beyond having a place for everything. It's also about finding balance, discovering places and people that renew your energy.

Lessons from Our Dog

His actions reminded us to appreciate those we love, enjoy every moment and embrace life enthusiastically.

NORTON, OUR BLACK LAB who passed away in the fall of 2005, inspired a series of organizing cartoons that first appeared in my newsletters and now in this book. These cartoons were based on actual situations. They were a creative collaboration between artist Richard Rockwell and me. Norton was a great friend that taught and inspired me in many ways. With his wagging tail and enthusiastic greetings, he gave us unconditional love. He was always ready for an adventure, whether it was running errands, walking down the block or taking a road trip. He never rushed and seemed to genuinely enjoy each moment, especially when it was spent with us. He loved people. What does any of this have to do with organizing?

An essential part of organizing is prioritizing and understanding what is important. Norton *definitely* knew what was important. He was a willing and eager participant in life. He also understood how just to *be*. Sometimes we'd rush around with our busy schedules, trying to fit in one more errand, make one more call, complete one more task, not giving ourselves enough time to be still. Norton was excellent at relaxing. Every once in a while he'd inhale and then exhale a deep, long, loud sigh. This helped us to stop, reflect, and breathe. I am grateful to have learned these essential life lessons from a great dog.

LaVergne, TN USA
27 October 2010
202445LV00005B/95/P